Life Of The Late John Elwes--

JOHN ELWES, ESQ.

THE LIFE

OF THE LATE

JOHN ELWES, ESQUIRE;

MEMBER IN THREE SUCCESSIVE PARLIAMENTS FOR

BERKSHIRE.

BY EDWARD TOPHAM, ESQUIRE,

Late Captain in the second troop of Horse Guards, and Magistrate for the counties of Essex and York.

FROM THE SECOND LONDON EDITION.

" *Every singular character merits some notice from pos-*
" *terity; and I have always said, that if fate prolong-*
" *ed my life, I would write his.*"

SHAFTSBURY'S CHARACT.

POUGHKEEPSIE:

PUBLISHED BY PARACLETE POTTER.

P. & S. Potter, Printers.

1815.

TO SIR PAUL JODRELL,

PHYSICIAN TO THE NABOB OF ARCOT,

AND NOW RESIDING IN INDIA.

My long valued friend,

THE life, which follows this, has already met more than its due share of approbation. But the singularity of the character will alone make it matter of curiosity. In delivering down to others an account so extraordinary, I was anxious to inscribe it with a name that might well deserve remembrance. A name of more merit than yours, I do not know; and should I here err, I am indeed mistaken in my judgment, for we have known each other during the period of our lives. We were boys together at ETON; students together at CAMBRIDGE; and we travelled together through SCOTLAND.

The distance which now divides us, removes from me all imputation of flattery here: and the usual homage of INDIA, will make you think what I am now saying of you, but very cool commendation.

This work, therefore, I inscribe to you as a tribute of long friendship; nor have I more to add, than to say, with submission, that while you are taking care of a NABOB, pray take care of YOURSELF.

EDWARD TOPHAM.

Cowslip Hall, Suffolk,
  January 20, 1790.

THE PREFACE.

DURING the life time of Mr. Elwes, I said to him more than once, " I would write his life." His answer was—" there is nothing in it, Sir, worth mentioning."

That I have been of a different opinion, my labours will shew; and if I have any knowledge of History, or Human Nature, it will form an epoch in the biography of the eighteenth century, that such characters lived as those of Sir Hervey, and Mr. Elwes, his nephew. Men voluntarily giving up all the blessings of life to save money, they knew not why; embracing poverty and mortification as the best lot of existence; and dying martyrs to that wealth, whose accumulation afforded no enjoyment.

In giving the life of Mr. Elwes to the world, such have been the sentiments that have filled my mind. The delineation of characters such as these, I consider as very moral instruction to mankind, and a lesson more demonstrative of the perfect vanity of unused wealth, than has hitherto been presented to the public; and such is the answer I give to those, who may have observed, " you need not have told all these things."

An observation so trivial as this, would have stopped, had it been regarded, every useful and improving narrative that time or History has delivered down to us. On such grounds even LIVY or Plutarch, had never written: the delightful Memoirs of SULLY, listening to such objections, had never seen the light: and all that aids virtue, or marks vice, by the presentment of recorded character, all had been sunk, without remembrance, or benefit to mankind !

Such have been my reasons for publishing the life of Mr. Elwes ; and I feel pleasure, that while I may have given those smaller traits of action which best delineate character, I can truly and conscientiously say, I have not omitted one circumstance in my memory, that was honorable to the man whose history I have written.

With this honest assurance, I present the Memoir, thus reprinted, to the public. Their approbation of it, more kind perhaps than just, has called for its republication.

On doing this, I give it as a voluntary tribute to a bookseller of merit and diligence ; and I wish him, unbenefitted myself, every success; but before I close this account, I ought not to omit the expression of my thanks to some members of the House of Commons, who favoured me with different anecdotes of Mr. Elwes, not entirely known to myself, and still more particularly to THOMAS RUGGLES, Esq. of Spains-hall, in the county of Essex, for the communication of some very beautiful verse, seen at the end of the Narrative.

THE LIFE

OF THE LATE

JOHN ELWES, ESQUIRE.

NUMBER I.

THE family name of Mr. Elwes was Meggot: and as his name was John, the conjunction of Jack Meggot, made strangers sometimes imagine that his intimates were addressing him by an assumed appellation. His father was a brewer of great eminence. His dwelling-house and offices were situated in Southwark; which borough was formerly represented in parliament by his grandfather, Sir George Meggot. Mr. Clowes is now in possession of the above premises. He purchased, during this life, the estate now in possession of the family at Marcham, in Berkshire, of the Calverts, who were in the same line. The father died while the late Mr. Elwes was only four years old; so, little of the character of Mr. Elwes is to be attributed to him; but from the mother it may be traced at once—for though she was left nearly one hundred thousand pounds by her husband—she starved herself to death!

The only children from the marriage above, were Mr. Elwes, and a daughter who married the father of the late Colonel Timms—and from thence came the intair of some part of the present estate.

At an early period of life he was sent to Westminster School, where he remained for ten or twelve years. During that time he certainly had not misapplied his talents—for he was a good classical scholar to the last—and it is a circumstance not a little remarkable, though well authenticated, that he never read afterwards. Never was he seen at any period of his future life with a book, nor has he in all his different houses now left behind him, books that would, were they collected together, sell for two pounds. His knowledge in accounts was still more trifling, and in some measure may account for the total ignorance he was always in as to his own affairs.

The contemporaries of Mr. Elwes at Westminster, were Mr. Worsley, late master of the Board of Works, and the present Lord Mansfield; who, at that time, had no objection to borrow all that young Elwes even then would lend. His lordship, however, has since changed his disposition, though Mr. Elwes never altered his.

From Westminster school, Mr. Elwes removed to Geneva, where he soon entered upon pursuits more agreeable to him than study. The riding-master of the academy there, had then to boast, perhaps, three of the best riders in Europe, Mr. Worsley, Mr. Elwes, and Sir Sidney Meadows. Of the three, Elwes was reckoned the most desperate: the young horses were always put into his hands, and he was the rough rider to the other two.

During this period he was introduced to Voltaire, whom he somewhat resembled in point of appearance : but though he has mentioned this circumstance, the genius, the fortune, the character of Voltaire, never seemed to strike him—they were out of his contemplation, and his way; the horses in the riding school he remembered much longer, and their respective qualities made a much deeper impression on him.

On his return to England, after an absence of two or three years, he was to be introduced to his uncle, the late Sir Harvey Elwes, who was then living at Stoke in Suffolk, perhaps the most perfect picture of human penury that ever existed. The attempts of saving money were, in him, so extraordinary, that Mr. Elwes, perhaps, never quite reached them, even at the last period of his life.

To Sir Harvey Elwes he was to be the heir, and of course it was requisite to please him. On this account it was necessary, even in old Mr. Elwes, to masquerade a little ; and as he was at that time in the world and its affairs, he dressed like other people. This would not have done for Sir Harvey. So the nephew used to stop at a little inn at Chelmsford, which he did not much like, and begin to dress in character—a pair of small iron buckles, worsted stockings darned, a worn-out old coat, and a tattered waistcoat, were put on, and onwards he rode to visit his uncle, who used to contemplate him with a miserable kind of satisfaction, and seemed pleased to find his heir attempting to come up with him in the race of avarice. There they would sit—saving pair !—with a single stick upon the fire, and with one glass of wine occasionally betwixt them, talking of the extravagance of the times; and when evening shut, they would retire to rest—as " going to bed saved candle light."

But the nephew had then what he had always—a very extraordinary appetite—and this would have been a monstrous offence in the eye of the uncle; so Mr. Elwes was obliged to pick up a dinner first, with some neighbor in the country, and then return to Sir Harvey with a little diminutive appetite that was quite engaging.

A partridge, a small pudding, and a potatoe, did the business! and the fire was suffered to go out while Sir Harvey was at dinner, as eating was quite exercise enough.

But as Mr. Elwes inherited from Sir Harvey a great part of the present fortune—somewhat of their histories becomes necessarily intermixed: and, I trust, a small digression to give the picture of Sir Harvey, will not be thought unamusing or foreign to the subject. He was, as may be imagined, a most singular character—and the way in which he lived was not less so. His seclusion from the world nearly reached that of an hermit: and, could the extremity of his avarice have been taken out of the question, a more blameless life was never led.

Of this character—a few singular circumstances shall be given:—and to the men of modern times and more dissipated manners, used to hurry, and accustomed to continual variety—such a system of living as he pursued, will scarcely appear credible. But the picture is real and curious. It will serve to show—" There is living out of London"—and that a man may at length so effectually retire into himself—that there may remain little else but vegetation in a human shape.

NUMBER II.

PROVIDENCE, perhaps, has wisely ordered it, that the possessors of estates should change like the successions of the seasons:—the harvest and the consumption of it—in due order, follow each other; and in the scale of events, are all necessary alike. This succession was exemplified in the character of Sir Harvey Elwes, who succeeded to Sir Jervaise, a very worthy gentleman, that had involved, as far as they would go, all the estates he received and left behind him. On his death, Sir Harvey found himself nominally possessed of some thousands a year, but really with an income of one hundred pounds per annum. He said, on his arrival at Stoke, the family seat," that never would he leave it till he had entirely cleared the paternal estate;"—and he lived to do that, and to realize above one hundred thousand pounds in addition.

But he was formed of the very materials to make perfect—the character of a MISER. In his youth he had been given over for a consumption, so he had no constitution and no passions. He was timid, shy, and diffident in the extreme; of a thin, spare habit of body, and without a friend upon earth.

As he had no acquaintance, no books, and no turn for reading—the hoarding up, and the counting his money, was his greatest joy. The next to that was—partridge setting: at which he was so great an adept, and game was then so plentiful—that he has been known to take five hundred brace of birds in one season. But he lived upon partridges—he and his whole little household—consisting of one man and two maids. What they could not eat he turned out again, as he never gave away any thing.

During the partridge season, Sir Harvey and his man never missed a day, if the weather was tolerable—and his breed of dogs being remarkably good, he seldom failed in taking great quantities of game. At all times, he wore a black velvet cap much over his face—a worn-out full dressed suit of clothes, and an old great coat, with worsted stockings drawn up over his knees. He rode a thin thorough-bred horse, and " the horse and his rider" both looked as if a gust of wind would have blown them away together.

When the day was not so fine as to tempt him abroad, he would walk backwards and forwards in his old hall, to save the expence of fire.

If a farmer in his neighborhood came in, he would strike a light in a tinder box that he kept by him, and putting one single stick upon the grate, would not add another till the first was nearly burnt out.

As he had but little connection with London, he always had three or four thousand pounds at a time in his house. A set of fellows, who were afterwards known by the appellation of the Thackstead gang—and who were all hanged—formed a plan to rob him. They were totally unsuspected at the time, as each had some apparent occupation during the day, and went out only at night, and when they had got intelligence of any great booty.

It was the custom of Sir Harvey to go up into his bed-chamber at eight o'clock, where, after taking a bason of water gruel, by the light of a small fire, he went to bed—to save the unnecessary extravagance of a candle.

The gang, who knew the hour when his servant went to the stable, leaving their horses in a small grove on the Essex side of the river, walked across and hid themselves in the church porch, till they saw the man come up to his horses. They then immediately fell upon him, and after some little struggle they bound and gagged him: they then ran up towards the house, tied the two maids together, and going up to Sir Harvey, presented their pistols, and demanded his money.

At no part of his life did Sir Harvey ever behave so well as in this transaction. When they asked for his money, he would give them no answer till they had assured him that his servant, who was a great favorite, was safe :—he then delivered them the key of a drawer in which was fifty guineas. But they knew, two well, he had much more in the house, and again threatened his life, without he discovered where it was deposited. At length he shewed them the place, and they turned out a large drawer, where were seven and twenty hundred guineas. This they packed up in two large baskets and actually carried off. A robbery which, for quantity of specie, was perhaps never equalled. On quitting him, they told him they should leave a man behind, who would murder him if he moved for assistance.

B

On which he very cooly, and with some simplicity, took out his watch they had not asked for, and said, " Gentlemen, I do not want to take any of you, therefore, upon my honour, I will give you twenty minutes for your escape ; after that time, nothing shall prevent me from seeing how my servant does." He was as good as his word: when the time expired, he went and untied the man ; but though some search was made by the village, the robbers were not discovered.

When they were taken up some years afterwards for other offences, and were known to be the men who robbed Sir Harvey, he would not appear against them.

Mr. Harrington, of Clare, who was his lawyer, pressed him to go to Chelmsford to identify their persons ; but nothing could persuade him. " No no," said he ; " I have lost my money, and now you want me to lose my time also."

Of what temperance can do, Sir Harvey was an instance. At an early period of life he was given over for a consumption, and he lived till betwixt eighty and ninety years of age.

Among the few acquaintances he had, was an occasional club at his own village of Stoke—and there were members of it, two baronets besides himself, Sir Cordwell Firebras, and Sir John Barnordiston. However rich they were, the reckoning was always an object of their investigation. As they were one day settling this difficult point, an odd fellow, who was a member, called out to a friend who was passing—" for heaven's sake step up stairs and assist the poor ! here are three baronets worth a million of money quarrelling about a farthing !"

When Sir Harvey died, the only tear that was dropped upon his grave, fell from the eye of his servant, who had long and faithfully attended him. To that servant he bequeathed a farm of 50l. per annum, " to him and to his heirs."

In the chastity and abstinence of his life, Sir Harvey Elwes was a rival to Sir Isaac Newton—for he would have held it unpardonable to have given—even his affections. And as he saw no lady whatever, he had but little chance of bartering them matrimonially for money.

When he died, he lay in state, such as it was, at his seat at Stoke. Some of the tenants observed, with more humour than decency, " that it was well Sir Harvey could not see it."

On his death, his fortune which had now become immense, fell to his nephew, Mr. Meggot, who by will, was ordered to assume the name and arms of Elwes.

Thus lived, and thus died, the uncle to old Mr. Elwes, whose possessions, at the time of his death, were supposed to be, at least two hundred and fifty thousand pounds, and whose annual expenditure was about one hundred and ten pounds!

However incredible this may appear, it is yet strictly true; his clothes cost him nothing, for he took them out of an old chest, where they had lain since the gay days of Sir Jervaise.

He kept his household chiefly upon game, and fish which he had in his own ponds; and the cows which grazed before his own door, furnished milk, cheese, and butter, for the little economical household. What fuel he did burn his woods supplied.

Those who have wished to find an excuse for the penury of Sir Harvey, have urged, that he had passed so long a period of his life alone, in recovering the estate, that he could not again encounter the world; and that his shyness was so extreme that company gave him no pleasure.

To those who are continually courting the bustle of society, and the fever of public scenes, it may be curious to learn, that here was a man who had the courage to live nearly seventy years alone!

That this was done without former scenes to afford matter for reflection or books to entertain, but in pursuing one ruling passion—the amassing of unused wealth.

To the whole of this property Mr. Elwes succeeded; and it was imagined, that of his own, was not at that time very inferior. He got too an additional seat—but he got it, as it had been most religiously delivered down for ages past. The furniture was most sacredly antique; not a room was painted, nor a window repaired; the beds above stairs were all in canopy and state; where the worms and moths held their undisturbed reign; and the roof of the house was inimitable for the climate of Italy.

In short, the whole verified what was said—"that no body would live with Sir Harvey Elwes if they could—nor could if they would."

NUMBER III.

THE contemplation of such a character as that of Sir Harvey Elwes, affords a very mortifying and melancholy picture of human infirmity. The contrast of so much wealth, and so much abuse of it, is degrading to the human understanding. But in return, it yet has its uses. For let those who fancy there is a charm in riches, able to fix happiness, here view all their inability, and all their failure; and acknowledge, that the mind alone " makes or mars" our felicity. For who would credit, that while the comforts, if not the luxuries of life, are supposed to confer happiness, and be the foundation of our pleasures; who would credit that Sir Harvey Elwes, possessed of two hundred and fifty thousand pounds, should live for above fifty years in solitude, to avoid the expence of company!—should deny himself almost fire and candle!—Should wear the cast-off clothes of his predecessor, and live in a house where the wind was entering at every broken casement, and the rain descending through the roof; voluntarily imposing on himself a condition little better than the pauper of an alms-house!

To this uncle, and this property, Mr. Elwes succeeded, when he had advanced beyond the fortieth year of his age. And for fifteen years previous to this period, it was, that he was known in the fashionable circles of London. He had always a turn for play, and it was only late in life, and from paying always, and not always being paid, that he conceived disgust at the inclination.

The acquaintances which he had formed at Westminster school, and at Geneva, together with his own large fortune, all conspired to introduce him into whatever society he best liked. He was admitted a member of the club at Arthu's, and various other clubs of that period. And, as some proof of his notoriety at that time, as a man of deep play—Mr. Elwes, the late Lord Robert Bertie, and some others, are noticed in a scene in the Adventures of a Guinea, for the frequency of their midnight orgies. Few men, even from his own acknowledgment, had played deeper than himself; and with success more various. I remember hearing him say, he had once played two days and a night without intermission: and the room being a small one, the party were nearly up to the knees in cards. He lost some thousands at that sitting. The late Duke of Northumberland was of the party, who never would quit a table where any hope of winning remained.

Had Mr. Elwes received all he won, he would have been the richer by some thousands, for the mode in which he passed this part of his life: but the vowels I. O. U. were then in use, and the sums that were owed him, even by very noble names, were not liquidated. On this account he was a very great loser by play; and though he never could, or perhaps would, ascertain the sum, I know from circumstances since, that it was very considerable. The theory which he professed, " that it was impossible to ask a gentleman for money," he perfectly confirmed by his practice;

and he never violated this feeling to the latest hour of his life.

On this subject, which regards the manners of Mr. Elwes, gladly I seize an opportunity to speak of them with the praise that is their due. They were such—so gentle, so attentive, so gentlemanly, and so engaging, that rudeness could not ruffle them, nor strong ingratitude break their observance. He retained this peculiar feature of the old court to the last; but he had a praise far beyond this; he had the most gallant disregard of his own person, and all care about himself, I ever witnessed in man. The instances in younger life, in the most imminent personal hazard, are innumerable : but when age had despoiled him of his activity, and might have rendered care and attention about himself natural, he knew not what they were. He wished no one to assist him—" He was as young as ever; he could walk ; he could ride; and he could dance ; and he hoped he should not give trouble, even when he was old."

He was at that time *seventy-five*.

As an illustration of this, an anecdote, however trival, may be pardoned. He was at this time seventy-three, and he would walk out a shooting with me to see whether a pointer, I at that time valued much, was as good a dog as some he had had in the time of Sir Harvey. After walking for some hours, much unfatigued, he determined against the dog, but with all due ceremony. A gentleman who was out with us, and who was a very indifferent shot, by firing at random, lodged two pellets in the cheek of Mr Elwes, who stood by me at the time. The blood appeared, and the shot certainly gave him pain; but when the gentleman came to make his apology and profess his sorrow—" My dear sir," said the old man, " I give you joy on your improvement—I knew you would hit something by and by."

In this part of his character, nothing could be more pleasant than was Mr. Elwes: it was the pecuniary part which ruined, as the Dramatist would say, " the stage effect of the whole thing."

Recurring, however, from this momentary digression to the subject which we left, (the scenes of play in which Mr. Elwes had been formerly engaged) it is curious to remark, how he then contrived to mingle small attempts at saving, with objects of the most unbounded dissipation. After sitting up a whole night at play for thousands, with the most fashionable and profligate men of the time, amidst splendid rooms, gilt sophas, wax lights, and waiters attendant on his call, he would walk out about four in the morning, *not* towards home, but into Smithfield! to meet his own cattle, which were coming to market from Thrayden-hall, a farm of his in Essex. There would this same man, forgetful of the scenes he had just left, stand in the cold or rain, bartering with a carcass butcher for a shilling! Sometimes when the cattle did not arrive at the hour he expected, he would walk on in the mire to meet them: and, more than once, has gone on foot the whole way to his farm without stopping, which was seventeen miles from London, after sitting up the whole night.

Had every man been of the mind of Mr. Elwes, the race of innkeepers must have perished, and post chaises have been returned back to those who made them; for it was the business of his life to avoid both. He always travelled on horseback. To see him setting out on a journey, was a matter truly curious; his first care was to put two or three eggs, boiled hard, into his great coat pocket, or any scraps of bread which he found; baggage he never took; then, mounting one of his hunters, his next attention was to get out of London, into the road where turnpikes were the fewest. Then, stopping under any hedge where grass presented itself for his horse, and a little water for himself, he would sit down and refresh himself and his horse together; here presenting a new species of bramin, worth *five hundred thousand pounds.*

The chief residence of Mr. Elwes, at this period of his life, was in Berkshire, at his own seat at Marcham. Here it was he had two sons born who inherit the greatest part of his property, by a will made about the year 1785. He failed not, however, at this time, to pay very frequent visits to Sir Harvey, his uncle, and used to attend him in his daily amusement of partridge setting. Mr. Elwes was then supposed to have some of the best setting dogs in the kingdom; their breed and colour were peculiar, they were of a black tan, and more resembled a hound than a setter. As a proof of their strength and speed, Mr Elwes once told me, that one of them, in following him to London, hunted all the fields adjoining the road, a distance of sixty miles.

On the death of his uncle Mr. Elwes then came to reside at Stoke, in Suffolk. Bad as was the mansion house he found here, he left one still worse behind him at Marcham, of which the late

Colonel Timms, his nephew, used to mention the following proof. A few days after he went thither, a great quantity of rain fell in the night; he had not long been in bed before he felt himself wet through; and putting his hand out of the clothes, found the rain was dropping through the ceiling upon the bed; he got up and moved the bed; but he had not lain long before he found the same inconvenience. Again he got up, and again the rain came down. At length, after pushing the bed quite round the room, he got into a corner where the ceiling was better secured, and he slept till morning. When he met his uncle at breakfast, he told him what had happened. " Aye! aye!" said the old man, " I don't mind it myself; but to those who do, that's a nice corner in the rain!"

On coming into Suffolk, it was that Mr. Elwes first began to keep fox-hounds; and his stable of hunters, at that time, was said to be the best in the kingdom. Of the breed of his horses he was sure, because he bred them himself; and, what never happens at present, they were not broke in till they were six years old.

In keeping fox-hounds was the only instance in the whole life of Mr. Elwes, of his ever sacrificing money to pleasure, and may be selected as the only period when he forgot the cares, the perplexities, and the regret, which his wealth occasioned. But even here every thing was done in the most frugal manner. Scrub, in the Beaux Stratagem, when compared with Mr. Elwes' huntsman, had an idle life of it. This famous huntsman might have fixed an epoch in the history of servants; for, in a morning, getting up at four o'clock, he milked the cows; he then prepared breakfast for Mr. Elwes, or any friends he might have with him; then, slipping on a green coat, he hurried into the stable, saddled the horses, got the hounds out of the kennel, and away they went into the field. After the fatigues of hunting, he refreshed himself by rubbing down two or three horses as quickly as he could; then running into the house to lay the cloth, and wait at dinner; then hurrying again into the stable to feed the horses; diversified with an interlude of the cows again to milk, the dogs to feed, and eight hunters to litter down for the night. What may appear extraordinary, the man lived for some years, though his master used often to call him " an idle dog!" and say, " he wanted to be paid for doing nothing!"

NUMBER IV.

IT has been remarked, that Mr. Elwes was one of the best gentlemen riders in the kingdom. Sir Sidney Meadows, who is the law upon this subject, always allowed it. His knowledge in horses was in no way inferior; and, therefore, while he rode before the whole county of Suffolk, the horses he rode were the admiration of every body. As no bad proof of this, he had offered him for one of his hunters the sum of three hundred guineas, and for another two hundred and fifty; a sum in those days almost incredible, when a very good horse might be bought for fifteen pounds.

To modern sportsmen, accustomed to warm clothing and hot stables, his manner of treating them may appear singular. As soon as they were perfectly dry after hunting, if the weather was clear, he always turned them out for two or three hours, let the cold be ever so intense. Thus they walked off the stiffness occasioned by fatigue, and preserved their feet; and to this he attributed their being able to carry him when one of them was twenty-two years old.

To Mr. Elwes, an inn upon the road, and an apothecary's bill, were equal subjects of aversion. The words "give," and "pay," were not found in his vocabulary; and therefore, when he once received a very dangerous kick from one of his horses, who fell in going over a leap, nothing could persuade him to have any assistance. He rode the chase through, with his leg cut to the bone; and it was only some days afterwards, when it was feared an amputation would be necessary, that he consented to go up to London, and, hard day! part with some money for advice.

No hounds were more killing ones than those of Mr. Elwes. The wits of the country used to say, "it must be so, or they would get nothing to eat." In truth it may be credited they lived but sparingly; though scarcely will it be believed by the Meynells, the Cokes, and Pantons of the present day, that the whole fox-hunting establishment of Mr. Elwes, huntsmen, dogs, and horses, did not cost him three hundred pounds a year!

In the summer, they always passed their lives with the different tenants, where they had, "more meat and less work;" and were collected together a few days before the season began.

During this time, while he kept hounds, and which consumed a period of nearly fourteen years, Mr. Elwes almost totally resided at Stoke, in Suffolk. From thence he made frequent excursions to Newmarket, but he never engaged on the turf.

A kindness, however, which he performed there, should not pass away without remembrance.

Lord Abingdon, who was slightly known to Mr. Elwes in Berkshire, had made a match for seven thousand pounds, which it was supposed he would be obliged to forfeit, from an inability to produce the sum, though the odds was greatly in his favour. Unasked, unsolicited, Mr. Elwes made him an offer of the money, which he accepted, and won his engagement. The generosity of the act no one will deny; but it was the fate of Mr. Elwes to combine some great actions with a meanness so extraordinary, that he no longer appeared one and the same person.

The anecdote which accompanied it, I had not long ago from a clergyman, on whose authority I can place the most perfect reliance.

On the day when this match was to be run, he had agreed to accompany Mr. Elwes to see the fate of it. They were to go, as was the custom of Mr. Elwes, on horseback, and were to set out at seven in the morning, Imagining they were to breakfast at Newmarket, the gentleman took no refreshment, and away they went. They reached Newmarket about eleven, and Mr. Elwes began to busy himself, in inquiries and conversation, till twelve, when the match was decided in favor of Lord Abingdon. He then thought they should move off to the town, to take some breakfast, but old Elwes still continued riding about, till three, and then four arrived. At which time the gentleman grew so impatient, that he mentioned something of the keen air of Newmarket Heath, and the comforts of a good dinner; "Very true," said old Elwes, "very true—so here, do as I do! offering him at the same time, from the great-coat pocket, a piece of an old crushed pancake, which, he said, he had brought from his house at Marcham, two months before, but "that it was as good as new."

The sequel of the story was, that they did not reach home till nine in the evening, when the gentleman was so tired, that he gave up all refreshment but rest! and old Elwes, having hazarded seven thousand pounds in the morning, went happily to bed with the reflection—he had saved three shillings! such were the extraordinary contradictions of this extraordinary man! But not amongst strangers alone, was money with him the dearest object of his life. He had brought with him his two sons out of Berkshire, and certainly if he liked any thing, it was these boys. But no money would he lavish on their education; for he declared, that "putting things into people's heads, was the sure way to take money out of their pockets."

From this mean, and almost ludicrous desire of saving, no circumstance of tenderness or affection; no sentiment of sorrow or compassion, could turn him aside. The more diminutive the object seemed, his attention grew the greater;

and it appeared as if Providence had formed him in a mould that was miraculous, purposely to exemplify that trite saying—"penny wise, and pound foolish."

That Mr. Elwes was not troubled with too much natural affection, the following little anecdote will testify. One day he had put his eldest boy upon a ladder, to get some grapes for the table, when, by the ladder slipping, he fell down, and hurt his side against the end of it. The boy had the precaution to go up into the village to the barber, and get blooded: on his return, he was asked where he had been, and what was the matter with his arm? He told his father that he had got bled—"Bled! Bled!" said the old gentleman, " but what did you give?"—" A shilling," answered the boy:—" Psha !" returned the father, " you are a blockhead! never part with your blood!"

From the parsimonious manner in which Mr. Elwes now lived, for he was fast following the footsteps of Sir Harvey, and from the two large fortunes of which he was in possession—riches rolled in upon him like a torrent.—And had he been gifted with that clear and fertile head, which, patient in accumulation, and fruitful in disposition, knows how to employ as well as accumulate—which working from principal to interest—by compounding, forms a principal again—and makes money generate itself; had he possessed such a head as this, his wealth would have exceeded all bounds. But nature, which sets limits to the ocean, forbade, perhaps, this monstrous inundation of property: and as Mr. Elwes knew almost nothing of accounts, and never reduced his affairs to writing—he was obliged, in the disposal of his money, to trust much to memory—to the suggestions of other people still more. Hence every person who had a want or a scheme, with an apparent high interest—adventurer or honest it signified not—all was prey to him; and he swam about like the enormous pike, which, ever voracious and unsatisfied, catches at every thing, till it is itself caught!—Hence are to be reckoned, visions of distant property in America; phantoms of annuities on lives that could never pay; and bureaus filled with bonds of promising peers and members, long dismembered of all property. I do not exaggerate when I say, I believe Mr. Elwes lost in this manner, during his life, full one hundred and fifty thousand pounds!

But perhaps in this ordination, Providence was all-wise. In the life of Mr. Elwes, the luxurant sources of industry or enjoyment all stood still. He encouraged no art; he bestowed not on any improvement; he diffused no blessings around him; and the distressed received nothing from his hand. What was got from him, was only obtained from his want of knowledge—by knowledge that was superior; and knaves and sharpers might have lived upon him, while poverty and honesty would have starved.

But not to the offers of high interest alone, were his ears open. The making him trifling presents, or doing business for him for nothing—were little snug allurements which, in the hands of the needy, always drew him on to a loan of money.—A small wine merchant who had these views—begged his acceptance of some very fine wine, and in a short time obtained the loan of some hundred pounds.

Old Elwes used ever after to say, " It was, indeed, very fine wine, for it cost him twenty pounds a bottle !"

Thus was there a reflux of some of that wealth, which he was gradually denying himself every comfort to amass. For in the penury of Mr. Elwes, there was something that seemed like a judgment from heaven. All earthly comforts he voluntarily denied himself; he would walk home in the rain, in London, sooner than pay a shilling for a coach; he would sit in wet clothes sooner than have a fire to dry them: he would eat his provisions in the last stage of putrefaction sooner than have a fresh joint from the butcher's: and he wore a wig for above a fortnight, which I saw him pick up out of a rut in a lane where we were riding. This was the last extremity of laudable œconomy: for, to all appearance, it was the cast off wig of some beggar ! The day in which I first beheld him in this ornament, exceeded all power of farce, for he had torn a brown coat, which he generally wore, and had been obliged to have recourse to the old chest of Sir Jervaise, from whence he had selected a full dressed green velvet coat, with flash sleeves: and there he sat at dinner in boots, the aforesaid green velvet, his own white hair appearing round his face, and this black stray wig at the top of all. A Captain Roberts, who was with us at the time, and who had a great respect for Mr. Elwes, was yet unable to sit at dinner for laughing.

When this inordinate passion for saving did not interfere, there are, upon record, some kind offices, and very active service, undertaken by Mr. Elwes. He would go far and long to serve those who applied to him; and give—however strange the word from him—would give himself great trouble to be of use. These instances are gratifying to select—it is plucking the sweet briar and the rose from the weeds that overspread the garden.

When Mr. Elwes was at Marcham, two very ancient maiden ladies, in his neighborhood, had for some neglect, incurred the displeasure of the spiritual court, and were threatened with immediate "excommunication."—The whole import of the word they did perfectly understand, but they had heard something about standing in a penance; and their ideas immediately ran upon a white sheet. They concluded, if they once got into that, it was all over with them; and as the excommunication was to take place the next day, away they hurried to Mr. Elwes, to know how they could make submission, and how the sentence might be prevented. No time was to be lost. Mr. Elwes did that which, fairly speaking, not one man in five thousand would have done; he had his horse saddled, and putting, according to usual custom, a couple of hard eggs in his pocket, he set out for London that evening, and reached it early enough the next morning to notify the submission of the culprit damsels. Riding 60 miles in the night, to confer a favor on two antiquated virgins, to whom he had no particular obligation, was really what no one man in five thousand would have done; but where personal fatigue could serve, Mr. Elwes never spared it.

The ladies were so overjoyed—so thankful: So much trouble and expence!—What returns could they make? To ease their consciences on this head, an old Irish gentleman, their neighbor, who knew Mr. Elwes' mode of travelling, wrote these words—" My Dears, is it expence you are talking of?—send him six-pence, and he gains two-pence by the journey !

NUMBER V.

THE character of an impartial and upright country magistrate is the best character which the country knows. What a lawgiver is to a state, an intelligent magistrate is, in a less degree, to the district where he resides. Such a magistrate was Mr. Elwes, while he resided in Berkshire; and it was almost totally owing to this best of recommendations, that an offer was made to him afterwards of bringing him in as representative for the county.

The prospect of a contested election, betwixt two most respectable families in Berkshire, first suggested the idea of proposing a third person, who might be unobjectionable to both parties. The person thus proposed was Mr. Elwes; and the county were obliged to Lord Craven for the proposition.

It was at this period that Mr. Elwes was passing, amongst his horses and his hounds, some rural occupations, and his country neighbors—the happiest hours of his life—hours which no future situation ever recalled—hours in which he stole from the perplexities which his wealth occasioned him afterwards; and where he forgot, for a time, that strange anxiety and continued irritation about his money—and that, which I know not how better to denominate, than by calling it the insanity of saving!

But as his wealth was accumulating fast, various were the people who were kind enough to make application to employ it for him. Some, very obligingly, would trouble him with nothing more than their simple bond—others offered him a scheme of great advantage, with " a small risk and a certain profit," which as certainly turned out the reverse—and others proposed " tracts of lands in America, and plans that were sure of success." But amidst these kind offers, the fruits of which Mr. Elwes long felt and had to lament, some pecuniary accommodations were not bestowed amiss, and enabled the borrowers to pursue industry into fortune, and form a settlement for life; and it is to be mentioned to the praise of Mr. Elwes, that in all the various sums which he lent, in the course of a long life, not one usurious contract or improper advantage taken, lives in the remembrance of any body.

This, in the conduct of a man living only to amass money, is peculiar praise; and while holding the pen of a faithful biographer, I am forced to recount circumstances I cannot commend—a most unpardonable omission should I esteem it, were I to omit the record of an action, that in some measure should shield this part of his character from reproach; which claims a merit, because the reverse might have been expected;

and proves that his avarice consisted not in hard heartedness, but in self-denial.

Mr. Elwes, from his father, Mr. Meggot, had inherited some property in houses in London; particularly about the Haymarket, not far from which old Mr. Elwes drew his first breath—for, by his register, it appears he was born in St. James's parish. To this property he began now to add, by engagements with one of the Adams, about building, which he increased from year to year to a very large extent. Great part of Marybone soon called him her founder. Portland-place and Portman square, the riding houses and stable of the second troop of life-guards, and buildings too numerous to name, all rose out of his pocket: and had not lord North and his American war kindly put a stop to this rage of raising houses, much of the property he then possessed would have been laid out in bricks and mortar.

The extent of his property in houses soon grew so great, that he became from calculation, his own insurer: and he stood to all his losses by conflagrations. He soon, therefore, became a philosopher upon fire: and I remember well, on a public house belonging to him being consumed, that he said with great composure—" Well, well, there is no great harm done: the tenant never paid me; and I should not have got quit of him so quickly in any other way."

In possessions so large, of course it would happen that some of the houses were without a tenant; and therefore, it was the custom of Mr. Elwes, whenever he went to London, to occupy any of these premises which might happen to be vacant.

He had thus a new way of seeing London and its inhabitants—for he travelled in this manner from street to street; and whenever any body chose to take the house where he was, he was always ready to move into any other. He was frequently an itinerant for a night's lodging; and though master of above an hundred houses, he never wished to rest his head long in any he chose to call his own. A couple of beds, a couple of chairs, a table and an old woman, were all his furniture; and he moved them about at a minute's warning. Of all these moveables, the old woman was the only one that gave him trouble, for she was afflicted with a lameness that made it difficult to get her about quite so fast as he chose; and then the colds she took were amazing! for sometimes she was in a small house in the Haymarket; at another in a great house in Portland-place; sometimes in a little room and a coal fire; at other times with a few chips which the carpenters had left, in rooms of most splendid and frigid dimensions, and with a little oiled paper in the windows for glass. In truth, she perfectly realized the words of the Psalmist—for though the old woman might not be wicked, she certainly was " here to day, and gone to-morrow."

The scene which terminated the life of this old woman, is not the least singular among the anecdotes that are recorded of Mr. Elwes. But it is too well authenticated to be doubted. I had the circumstance related to me by the late Colonel Timms himself.

Mr. Elwes had come to town in his usual way—and taken up his abode in one of his houses that was empty. Colonel Timms, who wished much to see him, by some accident was informed that his uncle was in London. But then how to find him was the difficulty. He enquired at all the usual places where it was probable he might be heard of: he went to Mr. Hoare's, his banker—to the Mount Coffee-house—but no tidings were to be heard of him. Not many days afterwards, however, he learnt from a person whom he met accidentally, that they had seen Mr. Elwes going into an uninhabited house in Great Marlborough street. This was some clue to Colonel Timms: and away he went thither. As the best mode of information, he got hold of a chairman—but no intelligence could he get of a gentleman called Mr. Elwes. Colonel Timms then described his person—but no gentleman had been seen. A pot-boy, however, recollected that he had seen a poor old man opening the door of the stable, and locking it after him; and from every description, it agreed with the person of old Mr. Elwes. Of course, Colonel Timms went to the house :—he knocked very loudly at the door—but no one answered. Some of the neighbors said they had seen such a man, but no answer could be obtained from the house. On this added information, however, Colonel Timms resolved to have the stable door opened, and a blacksmith was sent for—and they entered the house together. In the lower parts of it all was shut and silent. On ascending the stair-case however, they heard the moans of a person seemingly in distress. They went to the chamber—and there, upon an old pallet-bed, lay stretched out, seemingly in death, the figure of old Mr. Elwes. For some time he seemed insensible that any body was near him; but on some cordials being administered by a neighboring apothecary, who was sent for, he recovered enough to say—" That he had, he believed, been ill for two or three days, and that there was an old woman in the house, but for some reason or other she had not been near him. That she had been ill herself, but that she had got well, he supposed, and gone away."

On repairing to the garrets, they found the old woman—the companion of all his movements, and the partner of all his journeys—stretched out lifeless on a rug upon the floor. To all appearances she had been dead about two days.

Thus died the servant; and thus would have died, but for the providential discovery of him by Colonel Timms, old Mr. Elwes, her master! And let politicians hold forth, after this, on the blessings of a " land of plenty;" let moralists reason on the proper uses of wealth—and here shall they view an existing example which shall baffle all their theory. A mother, in Mrs. Meggot, who possessing one hundred thousand pounds, starved herself to death:—and her son, who certainly was then worth half a million, nearly dying in his own house for want!

With all his penury, Mr. Elwes was not a hard landlord, and his tenants lived easily under him. If they wanted any repairs, however, they were always at liberty to do it for themselves; for what may be styled the comforts of a house, were unknown to him. And what he allowed not to himself, it could scarcely be expected he would give to others.

Mr. Elwes had now resided about thirteen years in Suffolk, when the contest for Berkshire presented itself on the dissolution of the parliament, and when, to preserve the peace of that county, he was nominated by Lord Craven.

Mr. Elwes, though he had retired from public business for some years, had still left about him some of the seeds of more active life, and he agreed to the proposal. It came farther enhanced to him, by the agreement, that he was to be brought in by the freeholders for nothing. I believe all he did was dining at the ordinary at Abingdon; and he got into parliament for eighteen pence !

On being elected member for Berkshire, he left Suffolk, and went again to his seat at Marcham. His fox hounds he carried along with him ; but finding his time would, in all probability, be much employed, he resolved to relinquish his hounds ; and they were shortly after given away to some farmers in that neighborhood.

Though a new man, Mr. Elwes could not be called a young member, for he was at this time nearly sixty years old, when he thus entered on public life. But he was in possession of all his activity ; and preparatory to his appearance on the boards of St. Stephen's Chapel, he used to attend constantly, during the races and other public meetings, all the great towns where his voters resided. At the different assemblies he would dance amongst the youngest to the last, after riding over on horseback, and frequently in the rain, to the place of meeting.

A gentleman who was one night standing by, observed on the extraordinary agility of so old a man—" O ! that is nothing," replied another, "for

Mr. Elwes to do this, rode twenty miles in the rain, with his shoes stuck into his boots, and bagwig in his pocket."

NUMBER VI.

AT a period when men, in general, retire from public and fatiguing scenes, Mr. Elwes resumed them: and became an unexperienced member of Parliament, aged sixty. However opposite the whole of his life hitherto might have been to any thing that had the appearance of vanity, yet I have the testimony of many members of the house of commons, to assure me, he was not a little vain of his situation. And the facility with which various parliamentary gentlemen persuaded him for a time, to confer certain obligations on them, is some evidence that he once thought very highly of the honor of representation.

In three successive parliaments, Mr. Elwes was chosen for Berkshire: and he sat as member of the house of commons about twelve years. It is to his honor—an honor in these times, indeed most rare! that in every part of his conduct, and in every vote he gave, he proved himself to be what he truly was—an independent country gentleman. The character which Mr. Elwes supported in parliament, has been imitated but by few and excelled by none. For wishing for no post, desirous of no rank, wanting no emolument, and being most perfectly conscientious, he stood aloof from all those temptations which have led many good men astray from the paths of honor.

All that a minister could have offered to Mr. Elwes would have been of no avail: for posts or dignity would only have embarrassed him, by taking him away from the privacy he loved. As an instance of this, he was unhappy for some days on hearing that Lord North intended to apply to the King to make him a peer. I really believe, had such an honor fallen unexpectedly upon his head, it would have been the death of him. He never would have survived the being obliged to keep a carriage, and three or four servants—all perhaps, better dressed than himself!

For through every period of his life it was a prevalent feature in his character to be thought poor: that he could not afford to live as other people did; and that the reports of his being rich were entirely erroneous.

To these ideas he thought he gave strength, by having no servants, nor any of the "outward and visible signs" of wealth: and he had persuaded himself, that the public would really think he had no money, because he made no use of any.

Mr. Elwes was first chosen to represent the county of Berks in the year 1774—and he was brought in the way he best liked—at no expence. His brother member was Christopher Griffith, Esquire, who died in the year 1776, and he was succeeded by Winchomb Henry Hartley, Esquire, who was re-elected with Mr. Elwes, at the general election in the year 1780.

When Mr. Elwes first took his seat, the opposition of that time, headed by Mr. Fox, had great hopes that he would be of their party. Mr. Fox had that knowledge of him, which has joined many to his politics. He had seen him at Newmarket, and knew that he was fond of play ; and talked to him with that frankness which from great abilities and high political situation, is, and always must be conciliating. These hopes, however, were disappointed, in Mr. Elwes immediately joining the party of Lord North—and however it may now sound, it should be said, that let the public opinion of Lord North be now what it may, yet I am convinced, Mr. Elwes had no other motive for that union, than a fair and honest belief that the measures of Lord North were right. But Mr. Elwes was never of that decided and certain cast of men, that such a minister would best approve. He would frequently dissent, and really vote as his conscience led him. Hence, many members of opposition looked upon him as a man " off and on ;" or as they styled him, a " parliamentary coquette ;" and it is somewhat remarkable, that both parties were equally fond of having him as a nominee on their contested elections ; frequently he was the chairman ; and he was remarkable for the patience with which he always heard the council. In the longest committees, he seldom interrupted their harangues : and those gentlemen at the bar, who have most frequently put this virtue to the test, will remember his patience with gratitude. Of this great quality, to get through life, few men, if any, have possessed a larger share ; though in strict regard to truth, it may be added, he never had the good fortune to hear for one day—the trial of Mr. Hastings.

The honor of parliament made no alteration in the dress of Mr. Elwes ; on the contrary, it seemed at this time, to have attained additional meanness—and nearly to have reached that happy climax of poverty, which has more than once, drawn on him the compassion of those who passed by him in the street.

For the Speaker's dinners, however, he had one suit—with which the Speaker in the course of the session, became very familiar. The minister, likewise, was well acquainted with it—and at any dinner of opposition, still was his apparel the same. The wits of the minority used to say, " that they had full as much reason as the minister, to be satisfied with Mr. Elwes—as he had the same habit with every body."

At this period of his life Mr. Elwes wore a wig. —Much about that time when his parliamentary life ceased, that wig was worn out—so then, (being older and wiser as to expense) he wore his own hair—which, like his expenses, was very small.

Shortly after Mr. Elwes first came into parliament, he went to reside with his nephew, Colonel Timms, who then had a house in Scotland-yard. Of this nephew old Mr. Elwes was certainly very regardful, and indeed he had every cause to be so. —Those who had the honor of Colonel Timms' acquaintance while living, will not forget him now he is no more. The corps in which he served, remember him with regret; and the gentlemen of Suffolk, who were acquainted with him, looked forward, not without satisfaction, to a period when they imagined he would possess the property of Mr. Elwes—when he would reside among them—and when he would diffuse around the country those blessings great property can

D 2

confer, when it is used liberally! such blessings as spring from employing, improving, and civilizing the inhabitants of a country—such blessings as arise from the gracious purposes of hospitality and good neighborhood; and still more gracious purposes of relieving the distressed.

Riches thus employed, no person under Mr. Elwes had ever seen. Had Colonel Timms survived, I have no doubt such prospects would have been realised: an untimely death, however, cut off these hopes. The entailed estate which would have fallen to Colonel Timms, his son will inherit: and I doubt not, will find out, as the best part of his inheritance, the way to make the loss of a good father felt less severely.

Old Mr. Elwes still went on in his support of Lord North, and the madness of his American war, conducted as he conducted it, till the country grew tired of his administration. But the support of Mr. Elwes was of the most disinterested kind, for no man was more materially a sufferer. The great property which he had in houses, and those chiefly among the new buildings of Marybone, was much injured by the continuance of the war; and as no small proof of it, he had just then supplied the money to build a crescent at the end of Quebec-street, Portman-square, where he expended certainly not less than seven or eight thousand pounds, and which, from the want of inhabitants at that time, was never finished. It has since fallen to Mr. Baker, the ground landlord, who will doubtless make the money which Mr. Elwes lost.

Convinced at length of the ill conduct of Lord North, Mr. Elwes entered into a regular and systematic opposition to his measures, with the party of Mr. Fox, in which he continued till Lord North was driven from power, in March 1782. While the party were exulting in the scramble for places, and the division of the loaves and fishes—Mr. Elwes, with nothing to hope and nothing to fear, stood by with that honest indifference which characterises a man who looks not to men but to measures, and who votes only as his conscience bids him.

The debates at this period were very long and interesting, and generally continued till a late hour in the morning. Mr. Elwes, who never left any company, public or private, the first, always staid out the whole debate. After the division, Mr. Elwes, without a great coat, would immediately go out of the House of Commons into the cold air, and merely to save the expense of a hackney coach, walk to the Mount Coffee-house. Sir Joseph Mawbey, and Mr. Wood of Lyttleton, who went the same way as Mr. Elwes did, often proposed a hackney coach to him, but the reply always was, " he liked nothing so much as walking." However, when their hackney-coach used to overtake him, he had no objection to coming in to them; knowing that they must pay the fare. This circumstance happening so often, that they used to smile at this act of small cunning, and indulge him in it.

But as the satisfaction of being conveyed home for nothing, did not always happen, on those nights when it did not, Mr. Elwes invariably continued his plan of walking. A circumstance happened to him on one of those evenings, which gave him a whimsical opportunity of displaying that disregard of his own person which I have before noticed. The night was very dark, and hurrying along, he went with such violence against the pole of a sedan chair, which he did not see, that he cut both his legs very deeply. As usual, he thought not of any assistance : but Colonel Timms, at whose house he then was, in Orchard-street, insisted upon some one being sent for. Old Elwes at length submitted, and an apothecary was called in, who immediately began to expatiate on " the bad consequences of breaking the skin—the good fortune of his being sent for—and the peculiarly bad appearance of Mr. Elwes's wound." " Very probably," said old Elwes, " but Mr.———, I have one thing to say to you—in my opinion my legs are not much hurt ; now you think they are—so I will make this agreement : I will take one leg, and you shall take the other ; you shall do what you please with your's, and I will do nothing to mine : and I will wager your bill that my leg gets well the first."

I have frequently heard him mention, with great triumph, that he beat the apothecary by a fortnight.

All this time the income of Mr. Elwes was increasing hourly, and his present expenditure was next to nothing ; for the little pleasures he had once engaged in, he had now given up. He kept no house, and only one old servant and a couple of horses ; he resided with his nephew ; and his two sons he had stationed in Suffolk and Berkshire, to look after his respective estates : and his dress certainly was no expence to him ; for, had not other people been more careful than himself, he would not have had it even mended.

When he left London, he went on horseback to his country seats, with his couple of hard eggs, and without once stopping upon the road at any house. He always took the most unfrequented road—but Marcham was the seat he now chiefly visited; which had some reason to be flattered with the preference, as his journey into Suffolk cost him only two pence halfpenny, while that into Berkshire amounted to four-pence!

NUMBER VII.

WHEN Mr. Elwes thought he had got into the House of Commons for nothing, he had not taken into the account the inside of the house—the outside only had entered into his calculation. In a short time, therefore, he found out, that members of parliament could want money, and he had the misfortune to know one member who was inclined to lend them. Perhaps a fate ordained this retribution, and designed that thus only, some of the enormous wealth of Mr. Elwes should escape from his grasp. Be this as it may, there does however exist a pile of bad debts, and uncancelled bonds, which, could they be laid on the table of the House of Commons, would strike dumb some orators on both sides of the House.

In the survey of these monied memorials, it would seem as if some members had thought they were only franking a letter, or considered these bonds as a cover to go free.

Time, which conquers all things, conquered this passion of lending in Mr. Elwes; and an unfortunate proposal which was made him of vesting twenty-five thousand pounds in some iron-works in America, gave, at last, a fatal blow to his various speculations. The plan had been so plausibly laid before him, that he had not a doubt of its success; but he had the disappointment never to hear more of his iron or his gold.

From this period he began to think that the funds were full as safe as iron-works or members of parliament; and from that time he vested his money in those securities.

I have heard him say that three contested elections would not have cost him more than he lost by his brother representatives. In the year 1780, another member threatened him with a calamity not less likely to be afflictive. His neighbour, at that time, in Welbec-street, Lord George Gordon, gave him a prospect of diminishing his income upon houses; and as Mr. Elwes was his own ensurer, he passed his time very pleasantly during the fires. On a house adjoining to that where Mr. Elwes lived, being set on fire, Lord George Gordon offered, very civilly, to take the furniture of Mr. Elwes into his own house, by way of securing it. But Mr. Elwes full as civilly replied—" He was much obliged to his Lordship, but if he would give him leave, he would take his chance!"

On the dismission of Lord North, Mr. Elwes was left in the party with Mr. Fox; though he could not properly be said to belong to any set of men, for he had the very singular quality of not determining how he should vote, before he heard what was said on the subject. On this account he was not reckoned an acquisition by either side; and, it is but justice to say, he was perfectly indifferent to the opinions of both.

When the Marquis of Lansdowne came into power, Mr. Elwes was found supporting, for a time, his administration; and his Lordship will understand me, when I say—Mr. Elwes had his reasons to be satisfied with the peace; for he saw what he might not otherwise have seen.

Not long after this, Mr. Elwes followed his conscience upon a question and voted with Mr. Fox, against the Marquis of Lansdowne, and thus added another confirmation to the political opinion that was held of him—" That no man, or party of men, could be sure of him."

This was frequently the declaration of Sir Edward Astley, Sir George Saville, Mr. Powis, and Mr. Marsham, who all, and frequently, talked to him on his whimsical versatility. But it will, undoubtedly, admit a question, even in politics, how far a man, thus voting on all sides, as his opinion led him at the moment, be or be not a desirable man, in aiding the good government of a country.

Mr. Elwes having thus voted against the Marquis of Lansdowne, as a minister, went forward to assist, with his vote, the greatest monster in politics that ever disgraced any country since the beginning of time!—can any one have a doubt but I mean the coalition? an union so vulgarly atrocious---so contradictory to all the parties themselves had been saying but a few days before---and demonstrating, so plainly, the contempt in which they held all the common sense of the country, that, though I have talked with Mr. Elwes frequently upon the subject, I never could really learn why he supported it.

When he had quitted parliament, no man more reprobated this measure than he did: but I really believe he thought at the time, that Mr. Fox and Lord North were the only men able to govern the affairs of England. For had Mr. Pitt been then known to the world, the opinions of Mr. Elwes, as a man careful of large property, had been decidedly in his favour; for he has frequently declared to me since, and the declaration is curious and worth recording, because it is in the character of the man, and was in the outset of Mr. Pitt's political life:—" That after the experience he had had of public speakers and members of parliament, there was only one man, he thought, that could now talk him out of his money, and that was young Pitt!

With this coalition ended the parliamentary life of Mr. Elwes, who has continued firm in his support of it, and which was almost the only line of conduct he ever did support in parliament for any length of time. The character, however, which Mr. Elwes had long borne in Berkshire for integrity, might have made a re-election not improbable, notwithstanding the rage which had gone forth against all the abettors of the coalition and its principles. But here the private principles of Mr. Elwes stepped in, and prevented all thoughts of a contested election. Such a thing would have been so contrary to the saving features and very countenance of his character, that he would have died at the first election dinner. The usual parade of colours and cockades would have been to him a death-warrant, and open houses, at his expence, immediate execution.

Thus voluntarily, and without offer of resistance, he retired from parliamentary life, and even took no leave of his constituents by an advertisement. But though Mr. Elwes was now no longer a member of the House of Commons, yet, not with the venal herd of expectant placemen and pensioners, whose eye too often views the House of Commons as another Royal Exchange, did Mr. Elwes retire into private life. No: he had fairly and honourably, attentively and long, done his duty there, and he had so done it without "fee or reward." I say but what I aught: I write only that which I am in duty bound to write—when I here·set down—that a more faithful, a more industrious, or a more incorruptible representative of a county, never entered the doors of the House of Commons of England. In all his parliamentary life he never asked or received a single favour; and I believe he never gave a vote, but he could solemnly have laid his hand upon his breast and said, "So help me God! I believe I am doing what is for the best!"

Thus, duly honoured, shall the memory of a good man go to his grave: for while it may be the painful duty of the historian to present to the public the pitiable follies which may deform a character, but which must be given to render perfect the resemblance—on those beauties which rise from the bad parts of the picture, who shall say it is not a duty to expatiate?

The model which Mr. Elwes left to future members may, perhaps, be looked on rather as a work to wonder at, than to follow. The constituent becoming corrupt, renders the representative so of course. Where people will sell, buyers only can have goods; and the people will have themselves only to blame, when what is bought, is again sold.

Mr. Elwes came into parliament without expence, and he performed his duty as a member would have done in the pure days of our constitution. What he had not bought, he never attempted to sell—and he went forward in that straight and direct path, which can alone satisfy a reflecting mind.

In one word, Mr. Elwes, as a public man, voted and acted in the House of Commons as a man would do, who felt there were people to live after him; who wished to deliver unmortgaged to his children, the public estate of government; and who felt, that if he suffered himself to become a pensioner on it, he thus far embarrassed his posterity, and injured the inheritance.

Mentioning to me some years after his retirement his opinions of Mr. Fox and Mr. Pitt, he had this sentiment, always keeping true to the gold-colour of his character—" when I started in parliament, Mr. Pitt had not come into public life: but I am convinced he is the minister for the property of the country. In all he says there is pounds, shillings, and pence!"

Mr. Elwes, even in the support of the coalition, chiefly attached himself to the men of private good character in the party. Hence, the

Duke of Portland, Lord John Cavendish, were always favorites with him—and I have often heard him say, what to some may appear singular, " that there was not a better man of business in the whole house than Mr. Sheridan."

The late Mr. Byng used frequently to defend the principles of the coalition to Mr. Elwes. " Say it was convenient," replied Mr. Elwes, " and you express the cause better."

He was much pleased once with a remark made by sir Joseph Mowbey, who, together with Sir George Saville, were talking on that notorious act of union between Lord North and Mr. Fox. Sir George confessed frankly, it was expedient; for the friends of Lord North were so numerous, that Mr. Fox and his party could not go on without them. " Very true," replied Sir Joseph Mawbey, " that may be; but there is a difference between getting in and staying;—to preserve your place, you must preserve your character."

I have heard Mr. Elwes say, this was one of the remarks on the subject which he never forgot afterwards. And the propriety of the observation was fully justified by the event—for Mr. Fox has been ruined by the deed:—and Lord North saved nothing by it—but an impeachment.

By some it was suspected that the Duke of Portland had promised to do something for the younger son of Mr. Elwes, who was then a cornet in the second troop of horse guards. But I can safely clear him from this imputed attention to his son. There was nothing he thought less about, than a public life for him. He was against his ever purchasing into the guards—and only wished him to remain quietly a kind of steward for him in the country. Nay, so strong was his aversion to the act, that when this son, the present John Elwes, Esq. was first introduced to the corps, and when Lord Robert Bertie, who was then colonel, finding he was about to have the son of his former friend under him, desired to see Mr. Elwes—it was with the greatest difficulty he could be brought to the interview. Not all the scenes of former association, where they had so often met together, when the heart is young, and the imagination runs wild—when even dissipation affords more lasting cause for remembrance, and life is renewed again by memory—not all these could bring Mr. Elwes to an interview with any pleasure. The truth was, that in the actual possession of perhaps seven hundred thousand pounds, he was now living upon fifty pounds a year, and he did not wish his son to know he had lived otherwise.

NUMBER VIII.

THE national rage to see Mr. Pitt rescue this country from the odium that had attended it under Lord North and Mr. Fox, turned out Mr. Hartley as well as Mr. Elwes, from the representation of Berkshire. Mr. Hartley resigned his hopes not without reluctance; Mr. Elwes was terrified at once by the expence; and I am persuaded, if giving one dinner could have brought him in a second time, he would with all ceremony have begged to be excused. This unfortunate parsimony was certainly the chief cause of his quitting parliament; for such was the opinion his constituents entertained of his integrity, that a very small expence would again have restored him to his seat.

Nearly at the same time that Mr. Elwes lost his seat, he lost that famous servant " of all work"—compared to whom, Scrub was indolence itself. He died, as he was following his master, upon a hard trotting horse, into Berkshire, and he died empty and poor: for his yearly wages were not above four pounds; and he had fasted the whole day on which he expired. The life of this extraordinary domestic, certainly verified a saying which Mr. Elwes often used, and the saying was this—" If you keep one servant, your work is done; if you keep two it is half done; but if you keep three you may do it yourself." That there were very few kinds of work which this servant could not do, may be estimated by what he did: but that his knowledge of how some things were done, was not very extensive, may be taken from the following circumstance.

When the Dower House carried up their address to the King, on the subject of the American war, old Thomas, (for that was the name of the fellow) who had never seen his master do any thing but ride on his most important occasions, imagined he was to ride up to his Majesty at St. James's, and speak to him on horseback. Accordingly he cleaned up the old saddles, gave the horses a feed of corn at his own expense, and at his own expense too had a piece of new riband in front, put upon one of the bridles: and all this that his master might do things handsomely, and like a "parliament man!" But when he found out how his master was to go; saw the carriage of colonel Timms at the door, who, by borrowing for Mr. Elwes a big wig, lending him a shirt with laced ruffles, and new furbishing his everlasting coat, had made him look very differently from what he usually did, and in truth, much like a gentleman, old Thomas returning all his own zeal and finery back into the stables, observed, with regret, that "mayhap, his master might look a bit of a gentleman —but he was so altered, no body would know him."

During that very gallant stand which Mr. Pitt made with the House of Commons formed by another minister, and in which the rectitude of his conduct at length subdued all that friendship, or even dependance on others, could do against him, during this conflict, Mr. Elwes voted occasionally on each side; and he sometimes voted in a way, of which he afterwards saw the error. As an instance of this, he supported the India bill of Mr. Fox, and in a very short time afterwards he confessed he had been much deceived in the principles of that bill, and recanted his former opinion of it. Such accidents will not happen to those gentlemen who have epitomized parliamentary opinions upon every subject; and who might wish to vote first, and then hear what is said afterwards; but it may happen to that conscientious representative, who too hastily may give his assent at the time, and when he better understood the subject, hold a very different opinion. In this number Mr. Elwes was always to be reckoned.

Amongst the smaller memorials of the parliamentary life of Mr. Elwes, may be noted, that he did not follow the custom of members in general, by sitting on any particular side of the house, but sat as occasion presented itself, on either indiscriminately—and he voted much in the same manner.

During the whole time he was in the house of Commons, he never once rose to speak, or delivered his sentiments further than by his vote.

In his attendance at the house, he was always early and late: and he never left it for dinner, as he had accustomed himself to fasting, sometimes for twenty four hours in continuance.

When Mr. Elwes retired from parliament, no man ever retired from the House of Commons, leaving it more loaded with obligations than he did; and they were obligations that were never cancelled. If I might judge from the multitude of bonds I have seen, I should be led to think some members imagined he was a great public money lender, appointed by government to come down into the house of commons, and "oblige the gentlemen," who might be in want of his aid.

When application was afterwards made for the payment of them—on moving that question, Mr. Elwes stood as single as did the respected Mr. Strutt, member for Malden, on the subject of Admiral Keppel. Not a member said " Aye !" and Mr. Elwes died possessed of proofs most undeniable, that somehow or other, every man must pay for coming into parliament.

In these speculations, upon lending money Mr. Elwes was at one time most unbounded; the temptation of one per cent. more than the funds, or landed property would give, was irresistable. But amongst the sums he thus vested in other people's hands, some stray, forlorn instances of feeling may be remembered; of which the following is an instance;—When his son was in the guards, he was frequently in the habit of dining at the officers' table there. The politeness of his manners rendered him agreeable to every one, and in time he became acquainted with every officer in the corps; among the rest with a gentleman of the name of Tempest, whose good humor was almost proverbial. A vacancy happening in a majority, it fell to this gentleman to purchase; but as money is not always to be got upon landed property immediately, it was imagined some officer would have been obliged to purchase over his head. Old Mr. Elwes heard of the circumstance, and sent him the money next morning. He asked no security—he had seen Captain Tempest, and liked his manners: and he never once afterwards talked to him about the payment of it. On the death of Captain Tempest, which happened shortly after, the money was replaced. That Mr. Elwes was no loser by the event, does not take away from the merit of the deed; and it stands amongst those singular records of his character, that reason has to reconcile or philosophy to account for, that the same man, at one and the same moment, could be prodigal of thousands, and yet almost deny to himself the necessaries of life?

An anecdote, exemplifying the truth of this, I

will add at this moment. It comes to me on the very respected authority of Mr. Spurling, of Dynes Hall, a very active and intelligent magistrate for the county of Essex. It seems Mr. Elwes had requested Mr. Spurling to accompany him to Newmarket. It was a day in one of the spring meetings which was remarkably filled with races; and they were out from six in the morning till eight o'clock in the evening before they again sat out for home. Mr. Elwes, in the usual way, would eat nothing; but Mr. Spurling was somewhat wiser and went down to Newmarket. When they began their journey home, the evening was grown very dark and cold, and Mr. Spurling rode on somewhat quicker; but on going through the turnpike by the Devil's Ditch, he heard Mr. Elwas calling to him with great eagerness. On returning before he had paid, Mr. Elwes said— "Here! here! follow me! this is the best road!" In an instant he saw Mr. Elwes, as well as the night would permit, climbing his horse up the precipice of the ditch. "Sir," said Mr. Spurling, "I can never get up there." "No danger at all!" replied old Elwes; "but if your horse be not safe, lead him!" At length with great difficulty, and with one of the horses falling, they mounted the ditch, and then, with not less toil, got down on the other side. When they were safe landed on the plain, Mr. Spurling thanked heaven for their escape. "Aye," said old Elwes, "you mean from the turnpike. Very right; never pay a turnpike if you can avoid it!" In proceeding on their journey, they came to a very narrow road; at which Mr. Elwes, notwithstanding the cold, went as slowly as possible. On Mr. Spurling wishing to quicken their pace, old Elwes observed that he was letting his horse feed on some hay that was hanging on the side of the hedge—" Besides," added he, " it is nice hay, and you have it for nothing."

These pleasant acts, of endangering his neck to save the payment of a turnpike, and starving his horse for a halfpenny-worth of hay, happened, from the date of them, at the time he was risking the sum of twenty-five thousand pounds on some iron works across the Atlantic ocean, and of which he knew nothing, either as to produce, prospect, or situation !

Strange man ! whose penury and prodigality, whose profusion and meanness, all so mixed together, puzzle me still more and more, as I detail them to the public !

When Mr. Elwes quitted parliament, he was, in the common phrase, " a fish out of water !" Indeed, there is no trial more arduous, than that of acquiring, at an advanced age, new modes of life. To form new societies, and conciliate new friends, new spirits, alas ! are wanting. The style of Mr. Elwes's life had left him no domestic scenes to which he could retire—his home was dreary and poor—his rooms received no cheerfulness from fire ; and while the outside had all the appearance of a " House to be Let," the inside was a desert ; but he had his penury alone to thank for this, and for the want of all the little consolations which should attend old age, and smooth the passage of declining life. When he retired from Parliament, Mr. Elwes, as I apprehend, was nearly seventy-five years of age ; and the expenditure of a few hundred pounds would certainly have continued him in the situation he loved, where he was respected, and had due honour: where he was amongst his friends; and where long habit had made every thing congenial to him. All this he gave up to his love of money. That passion, which, consuming all before it, as it hurried him along the few remaining years of his life, at length carried him to his grave twenty years sooner than the muscular vigour of his body might have given reason to expect, for when Doctor Wall, his last physician, was called in, and viewed him extended on that squalled bed of poverty from which he would not be relieved, he said to one of his sons, " Sir, your father might have lived these twenty years, but the irritations of his temper have made it impossible to hope for any thing; the body is yet strong, but the mind is gone entirely!"

The scenes that now wait upon my hand, for the few years before his death, will exhibit a story of penurious denial with which it has never fallen to my share to find a parallel. In the wonder which they have yet left upon my mind, I can only say, "they are true!"

NUMBER IX.

MR. Elwes had for some years, been a member of a card club at the Mount Coffee-house; and, by a constant attendance on this meeting, he, for a time, consoled himself for the loss of parliament. The play was moderate, and he had an opportunity of meeting many of his old acquaintances in the House of Commons; and he experienced a pleasure, which, however trivial it may appear, was not less satisfactory—that of enjoying fire and candle at a general expense.

For however rejectful Mr. Elwes appeared of "the good things of this life," when they were to come out of his own pocket—he by no means acted in the same manner when those same things were at the expense of any other person. He had an admirable taste in French dishes, at the table of another—No man had more judgment in French wines when they did not come from his own wine merchant—and "he was very nice in his appetite," on the day he dined from home.

Much, therefore of his time, Mr. Elwes passed in the Mount Coffee-house. But fortune seemed resolved on some occasions, to disappoint his hopes, and to force away that money from him which no power could persuade him to bestow. He still retained some fondness for play, and imagined he had no small skill at picquet. It was his ill luck, however, to meet with a gentleman who thought the same, and on much better grounds; for a contest of two days and a night, in which Mr. Elwes continued with a perseverance which avarice will inspire, he rose a loser of a sum which he always endeavored to conceal—though I have some reason to think it was not less than three thousand pounds. Some part of it was paid by a large draft on Messrs. Hoares, and was received very early the next morning. This was the last folly of the kind, of which Mr. Elwes was ever guilty, and it is but justice to the members of the club, to say, that they ever after endeavoured to discourage any wish to play with him. Thus, while by every act of human mortification he was saving shillings and sixpences, he would kick down in one moment the heap he had raised.

Though the benefit of this consideration was thrown away upon him, for his maxim always was —and it was so agreeable, that he has repeated it to me at least a hundred times—" That all great fortunes were made by saving : for of that a man could be sure."

At the close of the spring of 1785, he wished again to visit, which he had not done for some years, his seat at Stoke. But then the journey was a most serious object to him. The famous old servant was dead ; all the horses that remained with him were a couple of worn out brood mares; and he himself was not in that vigor of body, in which he could ride sixty or seventy miles on the sustenance of two boiled eggs. The mention of a post-chaise would have been a crime,— " He afford a post-chaise, indeed ! where was he to get the money !" would have been his exclamation.

At length he was carried into the country, as he was carried into parliament, free of expense, by a gentleman who was certainly not quite so rich as Mr. Elwes. When he reached his seat at Stoke —the seat of more active scenes, of somewhat resembling hospitality, and where his fox hounds had spread somewhat like vivacity around—he remarked, " he had expended a great deal of money once very foolishly ; but that a man grew wiser by time."

The rooms at his seat at Stoke, that were now much out of repair, and would have all fallen in, but for his son John Elwes, Esq. who had resided there, he thought too expensively furnished, as

F

worse things might have done. If a window was broken, there was to be no repair but that of a little brown paper, or that of piecing in a bit of broken glass, which had at length been done so frequently, and in so many shapes, that it would have puzzled a mathematician to say " what figure they described." To save fire, he would walk about the remains of an old green-house, or sit, with a servant in the kitchen. During the harvest he would amuse himself with going into the fields to glean the corn, on the grounds of his own tenants; and they used to leave a little more than common, to please the old gentleman, who was as eager after it as any pauper in the parish.

In the advance of the season, his morning employment was to pick up any stray chips, bones, or other things, to carry to the fire, in his pocket—and he was one day surprised by a neighboring gentleman in the act of pulling down, with some difficulty, a crow's nest, for this purpose. On the gentleman wondering why he gave himself this trouble—" Oh Sir, replied old Elwes, it is really a shame that these creatures should do so. Do but see what waste they make! They don't care how extravagant they are!"

As no gleam of favorite passion, or any ray of amusement broke through this gloom of penury, his insatiable desire of saving was now become uniform and systematic. He used still to ride about the country on one of these mares—but then he rode her very economically; on the soft turf adjoining the road, without putting himself to the expense of shoes—as he observed, " The turf was so pleasant to a horse's foot!" And when any gentleman called to pay him a visit, and the boy who attended in the stables was profuse enough to put a little hay before his horse, old Elwes would slily steal back into the stable and take the hay very carefully away.

That very strong appetite which Mr. Elwes had in some measure restrained during the long sitting of parliament, he now indulged most voraciously, and on every thing he could find. To save as he thought the expense of going to a butcher, he would have a whole sheep killed, and so eat mutton to the—end of the chapter. When he occasionally had his river drawn, though sometimes horse loads of small fish were taken, not one would he suffer to be thrown in again, for he observed, " he should never see them again !" Game in the last state of putrefaction, and meat that walked about his plate, would he continue to eat, rather than have new things killed before the old provision was finished.

With this diet—the charnel house of sustenance—his dress kept pace—equally in the last stage of absolute dissolution. Sometimes he would walk about in a tattered brown coloured hat ; and sometimes in a red and white woollen cap, like a prisoner confined for debt.

When any friends, who might occasionally be with him, were absent, he would carefully put out his own fire, and walk to the house of a neighbor ; and thus make one fire serve both. In short, whatever Cervantes or Moliere have pictured, in their most sportive moods, of avarice in the extreme, here might they have seen realised or surpassed !

His shoes he never would suffer to be cleaned, lest they should be worn out the sooner.

But still with all this self denial—that penury of life to which the inhabitant of an alms house is not doomed—still did he think he was profuse, and frequently say " He must be a little more careful of his property." And strange as it may appear, I have no doubt he thought the resolve necessary, for his disquietude on the subject of money was now continual. When he went to bed, he would put five or ten guineas into a bureau, and then full of his money, after he had retired to rest, and sometimes in the middle of the night, he would come down to see if it was there. The irritation of his mind was unceasing. He thought every body was extravagant: and when some one was talking to him one day of the great wealth of old Mr. Jennings, and that they had seen him that day in a new carriage—" Aye, aye," said old Elwes, " he will soon see the end of his money."

It will be no exaggeration to say, that Mr. Jennings is supposed, by every man of business who knows him, to be worth a million. The remark therefore very curiously shews the mind of Mr. Elwes.

But strange as these anecdotes may appear, and indeed nearly incredible, it is my consolation to know that I write nothing but what is in the remembrance of various persons; and many of these occurrences passed under my own eye.

Of a character, therefore, so singular, who would not wish to know every thing ? and amongst traits so various, a theatrical anecdote may not be unamusing. It was during this period of his being in the country, that he first became acquainted with Mrs. Wells. The gallantry peculiar to the manners of the old court, led him to be very attentive and very ceremonious to her; and to the last moment of his life, she remembered the civilities which at times so distinguished him, and paid him every attention to the latest day in which she saw him.

As was natural, he would frequently talk to her about theatres; and she as naturally made mention of those present talents which adorn the drama of our day. She concluded he had seen Mrs. Siddons; No.—Mrs. Jordan? No.—Perhaps Mr. Kemble? No; none of them. It was probable then that he must have seen the stage of his own times—and remembered Mr. Garrick? No he had never seen him. In short, he had never been at a theatre at all! Thus, not amongst the least extraordinary parts of his character, had this extraordinary man let go by and pass without his notice, all that had been most gratifying to the national taste: all that a whole country had crowded to see; all that had been distinguished by public fame and honor; and all that must live while taste has a name amongst us!

And strong as may be supposed the desire must have been, to see some part of this, not once in the course of nearly eighty years, had the inclination been forcible enough to make him pay one crown for the sight. And Mr. Garrick, Mrs. Siddons, Mrs. Jordan, and Mr. Kemble all sunk before —five shillings! Is there in Great Britain, one man able to have seen these things, and living in the same town, of whom the same can be said?

Thus in every trait of his character, came forth the evil genius of money and spread its influence over all. In the close of that life to which I am hastening—well will it be, if the passion which undermined all the happiness of Mr. Elwes proves the means of destroying such a passion in others!

NUMBER X.

IT is the lot of some men to outlive themselves; and such was the lot of Mr. Elwes. When he first visited Suffolk, his peculiarities were but little known; and when he came to reside there, his fox-hounds " covered a multitude of sins." In leaving that county, to become a member of parliament, his public character they could not but praise; and in his private character, that which they did not see, they could not blame. But when he returned again into Suffolk, and exposed, to continued observation, all his penury—when his tenants saw in his appearance or style of living, every thing that was inferior to their own—when his neighbors, at best, could but smile at his infirmities—and his very servants grew ashamed of the meanness of their master—all that approached respect formerly was now gone. And a gentleman, one day enquiring which was the house of Mr. Elwes, was told, somewhat facetiously, by one of the tenants—" the poor house of the parish!"

The scene of mortification, at which Mr. Elwes was now arrived, was all but a denial of the common necessaries of life; and indeed it might have admitted a doubt, whether or not, if his manors, his fish ponds, and some grounds in his own hands, had not furnished a subsistence, where he had not any thing actually to buy, he would not, rather than have bought any thing, have starved; strange as this may appear, it is not exaggerated.—He, one day, during this period, dined upon the remaining part of a moor-hen, which had been brought out of the river by a rat! and at another, eat an undigested part of a pike, which the larger one had swallowed, but had not finished, and which were taken in this state in a net ! At the time this last circumstance happened, he discovered a strange kind of satisfaction, for he said to me— " aye! this was killing two birds with one stone !" In the room of all comment—of all moral—let me say, that, at this time, Mr. Elwes was perhaps worth nearly eight hundred thousand pounds! and at this period, he had not made his will, of course, was not saving from any sentiment of affection for any person.

As Mr. Elwes now vested the enormous savings of his property in the funds, he felt no diminution of it. He had given up the passion of *lending money*, entirely, for the last folly he was guilty of, in this way, was an offer of lending it to me; and, I must confess, he experienced an act of unkindness, to which he had not been accustomed— I did not take it.—The manner in which he offered it was not less singular. I was one day sitting reading in the room, and he was at a desk amongst his papers, which he left suddenly, and coming up to me, said—" pray, sir, would you wish to borrow a sum of money ? it is very much at your service, if you chuse it."—On my declining it, he looked astonished, and said—" well, now, I will never lend any money again !"—and, I believe, he was faithful to his word.

The spring of 1786, Mr. Elwes passed alone, at

his solitary house at Stoke; and, had it not been for some little daily scheme of avarice, would have passed it without one consolatory moment. His temper began to give way apace: his thoughts unceasingly ran upon money! money! money!— and he saw no one but whom he imagined was deceiving and defrauding him.

As, in the day, he would now allow himself no fire, he went to bed as soon as day closed, to save candle; and had began to deny himself even the pleasure of sleeping in sheets. In short, he had now nearly brought to a climax the moral of his whole life—the perfect vanity of wealth.

On removing from Stoke, he went to his farm house at Thaydon Hall; a scene of more ruin and desolation if possible, than either his houses in Suffolk or Berkshire. It stood alone, on the borders of Epping Forest; and an old man and woman, his tenants, were the only persons with whom he could hold any converse. Here he fell ill; and, as he would have no assistance, and had not even a servant, he lay, unattended and almost forgotten, for nearly a fortnight—indulging, even in death, that avarice which malady could not subdue. It was at this period he began to think of making his will—feeling, perhaps, that his sons would not be entitled, by law, to any part of his property, should he die intestate—and, on coming to London, he made his last will and testament, of which the following is an attested copy:

THE WILL OF THE LATE JOHN ELWES, ESQ.
Extracted from the Registry of the Prerogative court Canterbury.

"*In the name of* GOD, *Amen.*—I, JOHN ELWES, of Stoke, in the County of Suffolk, Esquire, do make and declare this writing to be my last will and testament, in manner following: (that is to say) in the first place, I direct that all my just debts, funeral, and testamentary expences, be paid as soon as conveniently may be after my decease. And I do give, devise, and bequeath, all and every my real estates, messuages or tenements, farms, lands, tythes, and hereditaments, situate, standing, lying, and being in the several parishes or places of Stoke, Thaydon, and Marcham, in the counties of Suffolk, Essex, and Berks, with all and every the barns, stables, outhouses, buildings, and appurtenances thereunto belonging; and all other my real estates whatsoever and wheresoever situate, standing, lying or being, with their and every of their rights, members and appurtenances; and also all and every my personal estate, goods, chattels and effects whatsoever, and of what nature, kind or quality soever, or wheresoever the same may be, unto my son, George Elwes, now living and residing at my mansion house at Marcham, in the county of Berks, and my son, John Elwes, late a lieutenant in his Majesty's second troop of horse guards, and usually residing at my mansion-house at Stoke, in the county of Suffolk, equally to be divided between them, share and share alike; to have and to hold all and every my said real and personal estates whatsoever and wheresoever, with the rights, privileges, and appurtenances thereunto belonging or appertaining, unto them my said sons, George Elwes and John Elwes, and their heirs, executors, administrators, and assigns forever more, equally to be divided between them as tenants in common. And I do hereby direct, that the executors of this my will do and shall, as soon as conveniently may be after my death, pay all and every such legacies or bequests as I may think fit to give to any person whomsoever, by any codicil, or paper writing in the nature of a codicil, or testamentary schedule, to be written or signed by me, whether the same shall or shall not be attested by any subscribing witnesses. And I do nominate, constitute, and appoint my said sons, George Elwes and John Elwes, executors of this my last will and testament; and hereby revoking all former wills by me at any time heretofore made, do make and declare this writing only as for my last will and testament. In witness whereof, I the said John Elwes have to this writing, contained in two sheets of paper, which I declare as and for my last will and testament, set my hand and seal, (that is to say) my hand to each of the said sheets, and my hand and seal to this last sheet and to the label by which they are affixed together the sixth day of August, one thousand seven hundred and eighty six,

JOHN ELWES."

" Signed, sealed, published, and declared by the said John Elwes, as and for his last will and testament, in the presence of us, who in his presence, and in the presence of each other, and at his request, have subscribed our names as witnesses to the execution thereof. FELIX BUCKLEY.
EDWARD TOPHAM.
THOMAS INGRAHAM."

" *November* 27, 1789—On which day appeared personally George Elwes, of Marcham, in the county of Berks, Esq. and John Elwes, of Stoke, in the county of Suffolk, Esq. and made oath, that they are the sons and executors named in the last will and testament of John Elwes late of Stoke. in the county of Suffolk, but at Marcham, in the county of Berks, Esq. deceased, who departed this life on the 26th instant.

"And these deponents further depose, that since the death of the said deceased, they have carefully and diligently searched amongst the said deceased's papers of moment and concern, for a codicil or other testamentary paper, which might be made and executed by him, the deceased, and referred to by him in his last will and testament hereunto annexed, and that they have not been able to find any paper writing whatever of a testamentary nature, save and except the last will and testament of the said deceased, hereunto annexed as aforesaid, bearing date the sixth day of August, in the year of our Lord one thousand seven hundred and eighty six.

GEORGE ELWES.
JOHN ELWES.

"The same day, the said George Elwes and John Elwes, Esquires, were duly sworn to the truth of this affidavit, before me,

   GEORGF HARRIS, Surr. Pres.
   JAMES HESELTINE, Not. Pub."

"Proved at London, the 27th of November, 1789, before the Worshipful George Harris, Doctor of Laws and Surrogate, by the oaths of George Elwes and John Elwes, Esquires, the sons and executors, to whom administration was granted, having been first sworn duly to administer.

GEORGE GOSTLING,
JAMES TOWNLY, } Deputy Register."
ROBERT DODWELL,

The property here disposed of, may amount, perhaps, to five hundred thousand pounds. The entailed estates fell to Mr. Timms, son of the late Richard Timms, Lieutenant-Colonel of the Second Troop of Horse Guards.

The sons, named by Mr. Elwes in the will above, were his natural children, by Elizabeth Moren, formerly his housekeeper, at Marcham in Berkshire.

In mentioning these gentlemen as " his natural children," my respect for them, I am sure will not be diminished: and a ring of no small value, lately sent to me by George Elwes, Esq. in the memory of their father, tells me I hold some place in their esteem. On the subject of natural children, what the facetious Dick Beckford once said so well, no man need be ashamed to repeat—" when so many *unnatural children* are *abroad*, I never shall blush to be called the *natural child* of my father."

A sentiment like this, will not misbecome the sons of Mr. Elwes: and as from the large property which has fallen to their share, some rank in society must be theirs also, that property will only be a benefit, or otherwise, as it is or is not well employed. In the person of their father, they have seen how small may be the advantage of enormous wealth; how little the happiness it confers, when confined: and that given to us for good or pleasurable purposes, for private or public ends, riches are a blessing, only as they are used.

If these hints be of service, their father will not have lived in vain: and that these hints shall not be disregarded, is their peculiar duty—for never yet has that prodigy been shewn to mankind—of one family being misers through three generations.

NUMBER XI.

MR. ELWES, shortly after executing his will, gave, by letter of attorney, the power of managing and receiving, and paying all his monies, into the hands of Mr. Ingraham, his lawyer, and his youngest son, John Elwes, Esquire, who had been his chief agent for some time.

Indeed the act was by no means improper. The lapses of his memory had now become frequent and glaring. All recent occurrences he forgot entirely; and as he never committed any thing to writing, the confusion he made was inexpressible. As an instance of this, the following anecdote may serve. He had one evening given a draft upon Messrs. Hoares, his bankers, for twenty pounds; and having taken it into his head, during the night, that he had over-drawn his account, his anxiety was unceasing. He left his bed, and walking about his room with that little feverish irritation that always distinguished him, waited with the utmost impatience till morning came, when, on going to his banker with an apology for the great liberty he had taken, he was assured there was no occasion for his apology, as they happened to have in their hands, at that time, the small sum of fourteen thousand seven hundred pounds!

However singular this act of forgetfulness may appear, it will yet serve to mark, amidst all his anxiety about money, that extreme conscientiousness which was to the honour of his character. If accident placed him in debt to any person, even in the most trivial manner, he was never easy till it was paid; and it should be noted, that never was he known, on any occasion, to fail in what he said. Of the punctuality of his word, he was so scrupulously tenacious, that no person ever requested better security; and he was so particular in every thing of promise, that in any appointment of meeting, or the hour of it, he exceeded even military exactness.

The summer of 1788, Mr. Elwes passed at his house in Welbeck-street, London; and he passed that summer without any other society than that of two maid-servants, for he had now given up the expense of keeping any male domestic. His chief employment used to be that of getting up early in a morning to visit some of his houses in Marybone, which, during the summer, were repairing. As he was there generally at four o'clock in a morning, he was of course on the spot before the workmen; and he used contentedly to sit down on the steps before the door, to scold them when they did come. The neighbours who used to see him appear thus regular every morning, and who concluded, from his apparel, he was one of the workmen, observed, " there never was so punctual a man as the old carpenter. During the whole morning he would continue to run up and down stairs, to see the men were not idle for an instant, with the same anxiety as if his whole happiness in life had been centered in the finishing this house, regardless of the greater property he had at stake in various places, and for ever employed in the minutiæ only of affairs. Indeed such was his anxiety about this house, the rent of which was not above fifty pounds a year, that it brought on a fever, which nearly cost him his life: but the fate which dragged him on thus strangely, to bury him under the load of his own wealth, seemed as resistless as it was unaccountable.

In the muscular and unincumbered frame of Mr. Elwes, there was every thing that promised extreme length of life, and he lived to above seventy years of age, without any natural disorder attacking him: but as Lord Bacon has well observed, " the minds of some men are a lamp that is continually burning;" and such was the mind of Mr. Elwes. Removed from those occasional public avocations which had once engaged his attention, *money* was now his only thought. He rose upon *money*—upon *money* he lay down to rest; and as his capacity sunk away from him by degrees, he dwindled from the real cares of his property, into the puerile concealment of a few guineas. This little store he would carefully wrap up in various papers, and depositing them in different corners, would amuse himself with running from one to the other, to see whether they were all safe. Then forgetting, perhaps, where he had concealed some of them, he would become as seriously afflicted as a man might be who had lost all his property. Nor was the day alone thus spent—he would frequently rise in the middle of the night, and be heard walking about the different parts of the house, looking after what he had thus hidden and forgotten.

Rest! thou perturbed spirit!—rest!

Is an apostrophe that here would have met real cause for its address—not in the wild fancy of the bard, bodying forth ideal forms and phantoms of the brain, but in the settled thirst after one object, forever preying upon the mind, and getting strange mastership over it. Then, as memory wore away, and reason became weaker and weaker still, exhibiting a wonderous picture of avarice rising over the ruins of the understanding; the mind all laid waste before it, and the body at length falling a sacrifice to feverish imagination. Preposterous passion! that " seemed to grow by what it fed on;" still more unsated when desire could have no room for want, and when the powers of enjoyment were all closed!

It was at this period, and at seventy-six years old, or upwards, that Mr. Elwes began to feel, for the first time, some bodily infirmities from age. He now experienced occasional attacks from the gout; on which, with his usual perseverance, and with all his accustomed antipathy to apothecaries, and their bills, he would set out to walk as far and as fast as he could. While he was engaged in this painful mode of cure, he frequently lost himself in the streets, the names of which he no longer remembered, and was as frequently brought home by some errand-boy, or stranger, of whom he had enquired his way. On these occasions he would bow and thank them, at the door, with great civility; but he never indulged them with a sight of the inside of his house.

During the winter of 1789, the last winter, Mr. Elwes was fated to see his memory visibly weakened every day; and, from the unceasing wish to save money, he now began to apprehend he should die in want of it. Mr. Gibson had been appointed his builder, in the room of Mr. Adam; and one day, when this gentleman waited upon him, he said, with apparent concern— "Sir, pray consider in what a wretched state I am; you see in what a good house I am living—and here are five guineas, which is all I have at present; and how I shall go on with such a sum of money, puzzles me to death—I dare say you thought I was rich; now you see how it is!"

In the spring of this year, the eldest son of Mr. Elwes, Mr. George Elwes, married a young lady, not less distinguished for her engaging manners than for her beauty. She was a Miss Alt, of Northamptonshire, and is the god-daughter of Mr. Hastings. She is indeed a lady of whom any father might be proud; but pride or even concern, in these matters, were not passions likely to affect Mr. Elwes, as a circumstance which happened a few years before, in a case not dissimilar, will prove:

Mr. George Elwes had, at that time, paid his addresses to a niece of Doctor Noel, of Oxford, who, of course, thought it proper to wait upon old Mr. Elwes, to apprize him of the circumstance, and to ask his consent. Old Mr. Elwes had not the least objection. Dr. Noel was very happy to hear it, as a marriage betwixt the young people might be productive of happiness to both.

Old Mr. Elwes had not the least objection to any body marrying whatever. "This ready acquiescence is so obliging," said the Doctor—"but, doubtless, you feel for the mutual wishes of the parties."—"I dare say I do," replied the old gentleman. "Then, Sir," said Doctor Noel, "you have no objection to an immediate union? you see I talk freely on the subject." Old Mr. Elwes had no objection to any thing. "Now then, Sir," observed Dr. Noel, "we have only one thing to settle: and you are so kind, there can be no difficulty about the matter; as I shall behave liberally to my niece—What do you mean to give your son?"—"*Give!*" said old Elwes, "sure I did not say any thing about *giving;* but if you wish it so much, I will *give my consent.*"

The word *give*, having stuck in the throat of the Elwes family for two generations—the transaction ended altogether.

That the above anecdote is literally a fact, Doctor Noel can testify, who that day discovered there was more than one short word in the English language, to which there is no reply.

The close of Mr. Elwes' life was still reserved for one singularity more, and which will not be held less singular than all that has passed before it, when his disposition and his advanced age are considered. He gave away his affections: he conceived the tender passion. In plain terms, having been accustomed for some time to pass his hours, out of economy, with the two maid servants in the kitchen; one of them had the art to induce him to fall in love with her; and it is matter of doubt, had it not been discovered, whether she would not have had the power over him to have made him marry her.

Had Mr. Elwes, at near eighty years of age and with property amounting to almost a million of money—thus closed his extraordinary life by a marriage in the kitchen, it would indeed have added one feature more to that singular memoir, which the life of this gentleman has presented to the public! and which, since the beginning of time, certainly never had a parallel!

But good fortune, and the attention of his friends, saved him from this last act—in which, perhaps, the pitiable infirmity of nature, weakened and worn down by age and perpetual anxiety, is in some measure to be called to account. At those moments, when the cares of money left him somewhat at ease, he had no domestic scene of happiness to which he could fly—and therefore felt with more sensibility, any act of kindness that might come from any quarter; and thus, when his sons were absent, having no one near him whom principle made assiduous—those who might be interested, too frequently gained his attention.

Mr. George Elwes having now settled at his seat at Marcham, in Berkshire, he was naturally desirous, that in the assiduities of his wife, his father might at length find a comfortable home. In London he was certainly most uncomfortable: but still, with these temptations before and behind him, a journey, with any expence annexed to it, was insurmountable. This, however, was luckily obviated by an offer from Mr. Partis, a gentleman of the law, to take him to his ancient seat in Berkshire, with his purse perfectly whole—a circumstance so pleasing, that the general intelligence which renders this gentleman so entertaining, was not adequate to it in the opinion of Mr. Elwes. But there was one circumstance still very distressing—the old gentleman had now nearly worn out his last coat, and he would not buy a new one; his son, therefore, with a pious fraud that did him honor, contrived to get Mr. Partis to buy him a coat, and make him a present of it. Thus, formerly having had a good coat, then a bad one, and, at last, no coat at all—he was kind enough to accept one from a neighbor.

NUMBER XII.

ON the day before Mr. Elwes took his gratuitous journey into Berkshire, he delivered to Mr. Partis that copy of his last will and testament, which he himself had kept, to be carried to Messrs. Hoares, his bankers. Mr. Partis punctually fulfilled his request, and this was the copy proved in Doctors Commons after the death of Mr. Elwes.

Mr. Elwes carried with him into Berkshire, five guineas and an half, and half a crown. Lest the mention of this sum may appear singular, it should be said, that previous to his journey, he had carefully wrapped it up in various folds of paper, that no part of it might be lost. On the arrival of the old gentleman, Mr. George Elwes and his wife, whose good temper might well be expected to charm away the irritations of avarice and age, did every thing they could to make the country a scene of quiet to him. But "he had that within" which baffled every effort of this kind. Of his heart it might be said, "there was no peace in Israel." His mind, cast away upon the vast and troubled ocean of his property, extending beyond the bounds of his calculation, returned to amuse itself with fetching and carrying about a few guineas, which in that ocean, was indeed a drop. But Nature had now carried on life nearly as far as she was able.—The sand was almost run out: for against such ceaseless inquietudes, what power of body could resist?

His very singular appetite Mr. Elwes retained till within a few days of his dissolution, and walked on foot twelve miles but a fortnight before he died.

The first symptoms of more immediate decay, was his inability to enjoy his rest at night. Frequently would he be heard at midnight as if struggling with some one in his chamber, and crying out, "I will keep my money, I will; nobody shall rob me of my property!" On any one of the family going into his room, he would start from this fever of anxiety, and, as if waking from a troubled dream, again hurry into bed, and seem unconscious of what had happened.

At other times, when perfectly awake, he would walk to the spot where he had hidden his money, to see if it was safe. One night, while in his waking state, he missed his treasure—that great sum of five guineas and an half, and half a crown! That great sum which he carried down into Berkshire as his last, dearest pleasure! That great sum, which at times solaced and distracted the last moments of a man, whose property, nearly reaching to a million, extended itself almost through every county in England.

The circumstances of the loss were these:—

Mr. Partis, who was then with him in Berkshire, was waked one morning about two o'clock by the noise of a naked foot, seemingly walking about his bed-chamber with great caution. Somewhat alarmed at the circumstance, he naturally asked, " Who is there ?" on which a person coming up towards the bed, said with great civility— " sir, my name is Elwes ; I have been unfortunate enough to be robbed in this house, which I believe is mine, of all the money I have in the world—of five guineas and an half, and half a crown!"—" Dear sir," replied Mr. Partis, " I hope you are mistaken; do not make yourself uneasy."—" O! no, no ;" rejoined the old gentleman ; " It's all true: and really, Mr. Partis, with such a sum—I should have liked to have seen the end of it.

This unfortunate sum was found a few days after in a corner behind the window shutter.

It was now the autumn of the year 1789, and the progress of each day took something away from his understanding. His memory was gone entirely ; his perception of things was decreasing very rapidly ; and as the mind became unsettled, gusts of the most violent passion usurped the place of his former command of temper. That courtesy, once so amiable in his manners and his address, was now conspicuous no longer ; and there appeared no particle of his mental qualities that did not seem to have survived themselves.

For six weeks previous to his death, he had got a custom of going to rest in his clothes, as perfectly dressed as during the day. He was one morning found fast asleep betwixt the sheets, with his shoes on his feet, his stick in his hand, and an old torn hat upon his head.

On this circumstance being discovered, a servant was set to watch, and take care that he undressed himself; yet so desirous was he of continuing this custom, that he told the servant, with his usual providence about money, that if he would not take any notice of him, he would leave him something in his will.

On the 18th day of November 1789, Mr. Elwes discovered signs of that utter and total weakness, which, in eight days, carried him to his grave. On the evening of the first day he was conveyed to bed—from which he rose no more. His appetite was gone—he had but a faint recollection of any thing about him ; and his last coherent words were addressed to his son, Mr. John Elwes, in hoping " he had left him what he wished." On the morning of the 26th of November, he expired without a sigh!—with the ease with which an infant goes to sleep on the breast of its mother, worn out with " the rattles and the toys" of a long day.

One strange circumstance I cannot here omit to mention :—some days previous to the death of his father, Mr. John Elwes was returning from an estate he had just purchased, in Gloucestershire, with a clergyman, to whom he had given the living. On his journey a strange presentiment came across his mind, that he should see his father but once again. The idea was so strongly impressed upon his thoughts, that he sat out in the middle of the night to reach Marcham; He did reach it, and was in time to be witness of that sight which most afflicts a good son, on the subject of a father—he beheld him expire.

Thus died Mr. Elwes, fortunate in escaping from a world he had lived in too long for his own peace!

I have now fulfilled my promise to the public; I have presented before their view the portrait of that extraordinary man, whose life will not hastily be forgotten in this country. In saying this I should indeed blush, could I take to myself any merit in the detail of it—No; I am free to say —it has not the smallest claim of that sort; but it is worthy some attention with the public, as being the faithful and accurate transcript of a man the most singular this country ever produced, long and intimately known to me, and whose manners, spite of some defects, I shall ever reverence and respect. For, it will happen, that the purest characters are not always those which are loved the most. A roughness of manner, and a temper that is imperious, will, forever, prevent affection, however highly we may think of integrity or virtue. In the mildness of Mr. Elwes's manners, and in the finished politeness of his address, there was more than a counterbalance for all his singularities. You esteemed him, perhaps, more than you ought; and even his faults seemed to spring from an infirmity that you pitied more than abhorred.

In giving his character, I have entered into the minutiæ, and all the little anecdotes of private life—for there, and there only, can the real character be seen.—Life when "full dressed," is always alike. It resembles the soldier on the parade, habited in one uniform, and acting with an uniformity that is equal to his habit.

The sentiment, which, doubtless, will arise in the minds of those who have perused this account will, perhaps, thus close with me, the result of all I have said.

Mr. Elwes, as one of the commons of England, in three successive parliaments, maintained a conduct which purer times might have been glad to boast, and which later times may be proud to follow. The minister that influenced him was his conscience. He obeyed no mandate, but his opinion. He gave that opinion as he held it to be right.

In one word, his public conduct lives after him, pure, and without a stain!

In private life, he was chiefly an enemy to himself. To others he lent much—to himself he denied every thing. But in the pursuit of his property, or the recovery of it, I have not, in my remembrance, one unkind thing that was ever done by him.

But that great object which rises highest to the view out of the prospect of his varied life—let me again enforce upon this page. That object is, the insufficiency of wealth alone to confer happiness. For who, after the perusal of the life of Mr. Elwes shall say—I am rich—and therefore I shall be happy?

Every circumstance of the memoirs here written, proves the fallacy of this hope. But still has such a life had its purpose. For if it should add

H

one circumstance consolatory to poverty—while it enforces the extreme and perfect vanity of wealth—then has such a life, as that of Mr. Elwes not been in vain.

Such be the wreath that my humble hand now strews over his grave; a wreathe where flattery has not furnished one single flower : but not wholly unadorned is it, for it is the tribute of truth ! As such, I give it to his memory ; and, at a moment, when praise or blame can affect him no more.

Supplementary to the above, I subjoin the following most beautiful inscription, as one of the very few literary compositions to which Mr. Elwes ever paid attention ; and it is to the credit of his literary taste. It was communicated to me by Mr. Ruggles, a very able and well informed magistrate for the county of Essex, who had it from Mr. Elwes himself; and the lines in Italics were marked by the pen of Mr. Elwes, as being peculiarly beautiful. They were written by the first Lord Hervey, a brother of the lady to whose memory they were inscribed.

TO THE MEMORY OF
LADY E. MANSELL,
NIECE TO THE MOTHER OF SIR HERVEY ELWES.

Vive pius, moriere pius! cole sacra! colentem
Mors gravis e templis in cava busta trahat!

Tho' the whole life should pass without a stain,
With PIETY, alike in health or pain,
To HEAV'N resign'd still DEATH shall be thy doom
And snatch thee from the ALTAR to the TOMB.

THE INSCRIPTION.

Beneath the covering of this little stone,
Lie the poor shrunk, yet dear, remains of ONE,
With merit humble, and with virtue fair,
With knowledge modest, and with wit sincere;
Upright in all the social calls of life,
The *friend*, the *daughter, sister*, and the *wife!*
So just the disposition of her soul,
Nature left reason nothing to control:
Firm, pious, patient, affable of mind,
Happy in life, and yet in death resign'd!
Just in the zenith *of those golden days,*
When the mind *ripens e'er the* form *decays,*
The *hand* of fate forever cut her thread,
And left the world to weep that virtue fled,
Its pride *when living and its* grief *when dead.*

THE LIFE OF

THE FOLLOWING

EPITAPH ON MR. ELWES,

Is copied from the Chelmford Chronicle. Its beauties, and the striking picture of the man whose memory it is intended to perpetuate, will be a sufficient apology for introducing it.

HERE, to man's honor, or to man's disgrace,
Lies a strong picture of the human race
In ELWES' form;—whose spirit, heart, and mind,.
Virtue and vice in firmest tints combin'd;
Rough was the rock, but blended deep with ore,
And base the mass—that many a diamond bore;
Meanness to grandeur, folly join'd to sense,
And av'rice coupled with benevolence:
Whose lips ne'er broke a truth, nor hands a trust,
Were sometimes warmly kind—and always just:
With power to reach Ambition's highest birth,
He sunk a mortal—groveling to the earth;
Lost in the lust of adding pelf to pelf,
Poor to the poor—still poorer to himself:
A foe to none, to many oft a friend:
Cold as to give, but generous to lend,
Whose wants, that nearly bent to all but stealth,
Ne'er in this country's plunder dug for wealth;
Call'd by her voice—but call'd without expense,
His noble nature rous'd in her defence;
And in the senate laboring in her cause,
The firmest guardian of the fairest laws
He stood;—and each instinctive taint above,

To every bribe preferr'd a people's love;
Yet still with no stern patriotism fir'd,
Wrapt up in wealth to wealth again retir'd.
By penury guarded from Pride's sickly train
Living a length of days without a pain,
And adding to the millions never try'd,
Lov'd—pity'd—scorn'd—and honor'd—Elwes died!
Learn from this proof, that in life's tempting scene,
Man is a compound of the great and mean;
Discordant qualities together ty'd,
Virtues in him and vices are ally'd :
The sport of follies, or of crimes the heir,
We all the mixtures of an Elwes share.
Pondering his faults—then ne'er his worth disown,
But in his nature, recollect thine own ;
And think—for life and pardon where to trust,
Was God not mercy, when his creature's dust.—

RECOMMENDATIONS

TO WILLETS' GEOGRAPHY,

Just published and for sale by P. Potter, Poughkeepsie.

The Rev. John Reed, A. M. Rector of Christ's Church, in the village of Poughkeepsie, has favored us with his opinion as follows—

"I have examined Mr. Willets' "EASY GRAMMAR OF GEOGRAPHY," together with the Maps accompanying it, and think it decidedly the best compendium of Geography for common schools yet presented to the public."

The Rev. CORNELIUS C. CUYLER, A. M. Pastor of the Reformed Dutch Church, in Poughkeepsie, has politely furnished us with the following recommendation :—

Poughkeepsie, 2d June, 1814.

Dear Sir,

I have given your edition of Mr. Willets' "EASY GRAMMAR OF GEOGRAPHY, for the use of Schools," together with the small Atlas accompanying it, as careful a perusal as time and other avocations would permit, and feel a pleasure in informing you, that it appears to be well calculated to facilitate to the young student, the acquisition of Geographical knowledge—I should therefore feel pleased to see it introduced into our schools. One of its principal excellencies is, that it will necessarily oblige the student to exercise other faculties besides his memory.

I remain yours &c.

CORNELIUS C. CUYLER.

RECOMMENDATIONS.

The Rev. JOHN M'VICKAR Rector of St. James' Church at Hyde-Park, has favoured us with the following note.

Hyde-Park, June 10, 1814.

Mr. Potter—At your request I have examined Mr. Willets' "*Easy Grammar of Geography,*" and think it the best, both in plan and execution, that I have yet seen.

J. M'VICKAR.

Mr. DANIEL H. BARNES, A. M. Principal of Dutchess County Academy, whose reputation as a public Teacher of Youth, stands as high as that of any man in the state, has politely communicated to us his opinion, in the following note—

Poughkeepsie, 2d June, 1814.

Mr. POTTER,

I have received a copy of your "EASY GRAMMAR OF GEOGRAPHY," and in answer to the request therewith communicated, I am happy to inform you, that the book, as to its plan and arrangement, meets my *entire approbation*. The method of placing the *exercises* immediately after each principal division of the globe, and making them include all the important facts previously laid down, appears to be admirably calculated to facilitate the rapid and correct progress of the students. The propriety of *closing* with astronomy is obvious. The maps are neatly executed, and being bound separately from the book, will be highly useful and convenient. I do not hesitate to say, that in my estimation, this compendium of geography, is preferable, as a *first* book, to any which I have seen. I shall adopt it immediately in my department, and recommend it to the other masters in this institution.

Yours respectfully,

D. H. BARNES.

RECOMMENDATIONS.

DAVID BROOKS, Esquire, well known to the public as having filled for many years the office of first judge of Dutchess County, and who has at different times been a member of the legislature of this state and of the United States, has obligingly favored us with his opinion, as follows:—

Mr. Potter—I have examined a small Tract, entitled "*An Easy Grammar of Geography, for the use of Schools,*"&c. with an Atlas of seven Maps, compiled by Jacob Willets, and published by you; and am fully of opinion that it will be a very useful elementary book for beginners in geography. The Maps, although upon a small scale, appear very accurate, and the lines *distinctly marked*. They afford a more correct idea of the *relative* situation of places, than those on a more extended scale; and being bound separate from the book, will be more durable and easy of inspection. I have no hesitation in recommending this book as a very useful *Compend;* and the moderate price at which it is afforded, puts it in the power of every scholar to procure it.

Wishing an extensive circulation to this useful little treatise, I remain, sir, your most obedient servant— D. BROOKS.

Poughkeepsie, June 1st, 1814.

Mr. John Griscom, a Teacher of the first respectability in the city of New-York, has favored us with the following note.

I have examined an "Easy Grammar of Geography" prepared by Jacob Willets, and do not hesitate to say, that the author, in my opinion, has fully attained the object he had in view; viz. to improve the popular little work of

RECOMMENDATIONS.

Goldsmith, and especially to adapt it more completely to the youth of this country. Thus improved, I consider it as one of the best Geographical compends for the use of American Schools, which has yet been published,

JNO. GRISCOM.

New York, 7 mo 9th, 1814.

Mr. ABIEL G. THOMPSON, who has been known in Dutchess county for many years, as a teacher of the first standing, and who is now one of the Instructors in Dutchess county Academy, has favored us with his opinion as follows:—

Mr. POTTER,

I have examined Mr. Willets' "EASY GRAMMAR OF GEOGRAPHY." It is in my opinion, a work better calculated for the use of schools than any book of the kind with which I am acquainted. It contains all that is necessary to be committed to memory in the study of Geography, and a great variety of questions, which the pupil may answer by examining the Maps.

The Atlas which accompanies the book, contains a number of Maps, sufficient to give a general idea of geography, and is a very useful appendage to the work.

Yours, &c.

ABIEL G. THOMPSON.

Mr. HENRY T. COOKE, one of the Instructors in Dutchess county Academy, has obligingly furnished us with the following note—

Poughkeepsie, June 2d, 1814.

Mr. POTTER,

Having examined "AN EASY GRAMMAR OF GEOGRAPHY," with the accompanying Atlas, published by you, and considering it a work of merit, I cheerfully recommend it to the use of schools, as well calculated to facilitate the progress of younger students in the important science of Geography. A system more concise, and that would at the same time answer all the purposes of the one now in use, has long been wanted.—Your publication I think, will tend greatly to obviate the difficulties attending the present method of instruction.

Yours, &c.

HENRY T. COOKE.

RECOMMENDATIONS.

Mr. E. W. A. BAILEY, one of the Instructors in Dutchess county Academy, has favored us with his remarks as follows—

Poughkeepsie, June 2d 1814.

Mr. Potter,

Having perused Mr. Willets' "EASY GRAMMAR OF GEOGRAPHY," together with the Maps, I can sincerely recommend it as a useful work, and better calculated to improve young beginners in the science of Geography, than any book of the kind, within the circle of my observation. The work appears to have been carefully compiled, and judiciously arranged. Yours &c.

E. W. A. BAILEY.

Mr. Andrew Beers, from whom the following note has been received, is now engaged in the arduous and important undertaking of writing a Gazetteer of his native state, Connecticut, similar in plan to Spafford's.

DANBURY, 14th July 1814.

Mr. Potter,

SIR—I have thoroughly examined Mr. Willets' *"Easy Grammar of Geography"* with the accompanying Atlas, published by you; and I might with much propriety (if needful) enter into the particulars of its high merits and great utility: but suffice it to say, that I have been an old teacher, in the usual mode of Geography and Astronomy, and I am now constrained to say, that I regret the many days, months, and I may even say years, I have spent in teaching according to the usual Books, only for the want of just such a one as you have hit upon. For young pupils it certainly exceeds any thing of the kind I ever saw. To study Geography and Astronomy without *Maps, Figures,* &c. is as absurd as to teach a child to call over the Alphabet without seeing the shape of the letters. The convenience of having the Atlas by itself is obvious, as it must be constantly used in search for an answer to every question, which I readily conceive will be a kind of pleasing labour to the scholar, and soon make him a proficient in Geography.

Yours &c.

ANDREW BEERS.

RECOMMENDATIONS.

The following letter is from the author of the Gazetteer of the State of New-York.

Albany, 7th Mo. 4, 1814.

Esteemed Friend,
  I have examined thy "EASY GRAMMAR OF GEOGRAPHY" and the 'ATLAS,' with some care. For an elementary book, in common schools, the plan meets my entire approbation; and so far as I have been able to observe, it is very well executed. Being a cheap and useful book, it ought to, and probably will, find its way into every school in the state. I had been long since solicited, by several persons employed in the instruction of youth, to write a work of this kind, on the same plan, and am very happy to see that my prospective labor may be dispensed with. Wishing thee very great success in thy literary enterprise,
    I remain thy friend,
      HORATIO GATES SPAFFORD.
Paraclete Potter.

Mr. R. O. K. BENNETT, from whom the following letter has been received, is a teacher of the first standing and respectability, who has for many years been employed in the city of Albany.

ALBANY, June 24, 1814.
Dear Sir—Your "*Easy Grammar of Geography,*" and accompanying Atlas, have been duly received. As an elementary book, it is justly entitled to a preference to any I have seen on the subject. It supplies what has long been wanting in common schools and academies, and what I have frequently heard called for—an easy epitome of Geography, at a moderate price, and on a plan calculated to exercise the ingenuity, as well as the memory of pupils. Thoroughly convinced of its utility, I shall lose no time in introducing it into my school; and shall be much rejoiced to find it soon in general use. The astonishing and truly gratifying changes which have taken place in the political aspect of Europe, will render it necessary for the compiler to make in a second edition (which I hope a

RECOMMENDATIONS.

discerning public will soon call for) some trifling alterations. Wishing you all the success to which the merits of this book justly entitle you, I remain,

Your obliged humble servant,

R. O. K. BENNETT.

Mr. P. POTTER.

RECOMMENDATIONS.

discerning public will soon call for) some trifling alterations. Wishing you all the success to which the merits of this book justly entitle you, I remain,
Your obliged humble servant,
R. O. K. BENNETT.

Mr. P. POTTER.

Lightning Source UK Ltd.
Milton Keynes UK
UKHW020301081222
413533UK00006B/262